I0820865

India in a Bowl

Megha Kohli

India in a Bowl

COMPLETE INDIAN MEALS, THE EASY WAY

MEGHA KOHLI

Photographs
ANSHIKA VARMA

ROLI

Getting Started

India's culinary landscape is as vast and varied as its people, and for me, it has been a lifelong love affair – one that began in my Dadi's kitchen, watching her create magic with simple ingredients. My culinary career has taken me from luxury hotel kitchens to running my own restaurant and consultancy, but at the heart of it all is my belief that food should be nourishing, sustainable, simple and deeply personal. Over the years, as I trained in some of the finest kitchens and travelled across the country, I found myself drawn to the food that brings us comfort – the kind that nourishes the soul as much as it satisfies the palate. *India in a Bowl* is an ode to these heart-warming meals, celebrating the flavours and traditions that have shaped my journey as a chef.

In this book, I show you how to make a wide range of Indian food, from simple every day fare to slightly more complex, elevated meals. I want to reassure you that making a delicious meal is something everyone is capable of. **For first-timers, a word of counsel: Don't let the number of components that make up each bowl intimidate you.** For Indian food, there is a set eating style, where we eat our rice, roti or grains along with curries and pair them with chutneys, raitas or salads. In the bowls I have prepared, I have set out a few dishes that pair well, but you don't have to make them all. They are suggestions, not rigid directives, so feel free to pick and choose depending on how much time you have, how hungry you are and what is available in your fridge – most of the mains and quite a few of the sides can be eaten on their own as a meal.

A word of advice, **make the investment in buying a few essential spices,** which forms the base of Indian flavours. With that out of the way, most of these recipes are fairly simple in technique and therefore easy to master. And once, you are familiar with the recipes remember to make them your own – add more spice, change up the flavours or add your choice of protein.

Now, as for how much time these recipes may take to cook. **I will concede that cooking takes time, but it will be worth it. I have provided tips and tricks on how to prep ahead and make these recipes time-efficient. You can plan and prep ahead so that you can be efficient in putting together bowls that are balanced, complete meals.** Most foods can be cooked ahead in big batches and stored in the refrigerator, or kept frozen until you are ready to use them. Knowing which foods can be prepped ahead of cooking them, can mean a bit of leisurely cooking on less harried afternoons, reducing the active cooking time for most of the recipes and allowing you to have ready the building blocks of quick, nutritious meals. As you make your shopping lists, read through the recipes to see which foods can be cooked in batches to reduce prep time during the week.

Beyond individual dishes, India in a Bowl shows you how to build a wholesome meal that is easy to put together. Indian food is deeply rooted in the idea of complementary flavours – a rich curry paired with a cooling raita, a crisp papad adding texture to a soft, buttery dal. While this book offers combinations that work harmoniously together, **each dish also stands on its own, allowing you to mix and match effortlessly. And as you get familiar with the broad range of recipes in the book, have fun building your own bowl.** Pick a grain, pair it with a protein and add a side or two, and you have got yourself a delicious bowl that is a balanced blend of flavours and food groups.

These meals have been designed to accommodate our busy and complicated lives, yet the book recognizes the need to eat well. Whether you are cooking for yourself or looking for meal ideas for family meals where you have to accommodate varying eating preferences, the book has something for everyone. It includes a variety of options from all food groups that will enhance the eating experience for even the pickiest eaters.

While the recipes in this book are inspired by regional specialties and nostalgic flavours, they are designed for modern kitchens and contemporary lifestyles. I have reimagined traditional dishes with effortless techniques, ensuring that they remain bold in taste yet simple to recreate. Whether you're coming home after a long workday, planning a cosy family dinner or prepping a solo meal, these recipes bring the essence of Indian comfort food into your bowl with minimal fuss. With this book, I invite you to experience the joy of Indian home cooking—one bowl at a time.

1

Rice

Cooked rice can be kept in an airtight container in the fridge and safely consumed for 3–4 days. Frozen, cooked rice can be stored for 1 month. Take care to reheat the thawed rice thoroughly.

3

Fish and Meat

If possible, marinate fish or meat the night before you plan to cook it. Marinating meat tenderizes the protein and allows the ingredients to seep into it, intensifying the flavour. Frozen, marinated meat can last up to 2 months. When you are ready to use the marinated meat, remember to thaw it in the refrigerator.

2

Pulses and Legumes

Soak pulses and legumes overnight, and cook them. Cool them completely, store in airtight containers and refrigerate. They last 5–7 days in the refrigerator. If you would like to store your cooked lentils longer, you can freeze them in ready-to-eat portions – they will last up to 3 months frozen.

4

Grains

Pre-cook grains like millets, barley or quinoa and refrigerate for 3–4 days. You can cook them in big batches and freeze them in ready-to-eat portions for 1 month. Cook these grains al dente, to prevent them from getting overcooked when you reheat them.

5

Dosa/Idli Batter

Ferment a large batch of dosa/idli batter and store in an airtight container for up to 3 days in the refrigerator. Store-bought dosa/idli batter is a great alternative to the fuss of homemade batter, and lasts for the same amount of time in the refrigerator.

6

Ginger-garlic Paste

To make a batch of ginger-garlic paste, add equal weights of ginger and garlic in a food processor and blitz to a smooth paste. Store the paste in a glass container with an airtight lid. Add 1–2 Tbsp cooking oil to the top of the ginger-garlic paste to increase its shelf life. Homemade ginger-garlic paste lasts 2–3 weeks in the refrigerator. Always use a clean, dry spoon to scoop out your ginger-garlic paste. You can also freeze ginger-garlic paste in ready-to-use portions for up to 2 months.

7

Brown Onion Paste

A key ingredient in Indian curries, brown onion paste is used to thicken curries and enhance their flavour. To prepare a big batch of brown onion paste, fry 1 kg thinly-sliced onions in 3–4 cups cooking oil. After 10 minutes of cooking the onions, add 1 tsp salt to help cook them faster. Once the onions have browned and caramelized, allow them to cool. Add the onions to a food processor and blitz to a smooth paste. To freeze, portion them into ice cube trays and freeze until solid. Add the cubes to a freezable bag and store for up to 3 months.

8

Dressings

Homemade salad dressings can be prepped ahead of time, and stored in airtight glass jars in the fridge for 3–4 days. Vinaigrettes last longer than creamy dressings.

9

Birista

Thinly sliced fried onions are must-have pantry staple for cooking Indian food. Added to biryanis, kebabs and kormas, or sprinkle over a dish of your choice. To prepare a big batch of birista, fry 1 kg thinly-sliced onions in batches, in 4–5 cups cooking oil. Place the fried onions on kitchen paper-lined plates to drain the excess oil. Birista can be stored in the refrigerator in an airtight container for 4–5 days, without turning rancid. Frozen, birista can last up to 6 months.

10

Coriander Powder

An essential spice in Indian cooking is roasted coriander powder. Dry roast the coriander seeds until they turn light brown and fragrant. Cool, then add to a food processor, and blitz to a powder. Store this in an airtight jar.

11

Cumin Powder

One of the most commonly used spices in Indian cooking is roasted cumin powder. Dry roast the cumin seeds until they turn dark brown and fragrant. Cool, then add to a food processor, and blitz to a powder. Store this in an airtight jar.

12

Hung Yoghurt

A common pantry staple for Indian cooking, hung yoghurt is made by straining all the whey from it. To make hung yoghurt set up a deep bowl and place a muslin cloth-lined strainer over it. The strainer should not touch the bottom of the bowl, as the whey will collect into it. Add the yoghurt, and knot the 4 edges of the muslin cloth together, to create a bundle. Now, add a weight above the muslin bundle and let it rest in your fridge overnight. All the whey will be drained out and you will have creamy hung yoghurt.

13

Vegetables

Blanch your hardy, fibrous vegetables and once cooled store them in airtight containers and refrigerate for 3–4 days. Blanching vegetables like green beans, broccoli, or even cauliflower ensures a shorter cook time, yet tender vegetables. And if you have ever felt like cooking your vegetables to desired doneness is taking a little too much oil, turn to blanching them first.

Happy Cooking!

Chutneys and Dips

Mint Yoghurt
Hummus
Coriander Salsa
Beetroot Yoghurt
Aam Ki Launji
Raw Mango Salsa
Doon Chetin
Burani Raita

Lehsun Mirchi Chutney

Mango Chutney

Green Coconut Chutney

Green Garlic Chutney

Coconut Chutney

Litchi Mirchi Chutney

Tomato Jaggery Chutney

Pudina Dhania Chutney

Coconut Chutney

Preparation Time
15 mins

Makes
150 gm

Ingredients

1½ Tbsp Bengal gram (chana dal), split
½ cup Grated fresh coconut
2 Small green chillies
½-inch Ginger piece
Salt, to taste
¼ cup Water
1 Tbsp Coconut oil
1 tsp Black mustard seeds
1 tsp Black gram (urad dal), Split and skinned
1 Dried red chilli
5–8 Curry leaves
1 tsp Fenugreek seeds

Method

1. Place the chana dal in a pan on low heat and roast for 2–3 minutes. Set aside.
2. Place the coconut, chana dal, green chillies, ginger, salt and ¼ cup water in a food processor and blitz to a coarse paste. Transfer the paste into a bowl and set aside.
3. Heat the coconut oil in a pan over medium heat. Once the oil is hot, add the mustard seeds and urad dal; sauté for 30–45 seconds.
4. Add in the red chilli, curry leaves and fenugreek seeds, and fry for 30–45 seconds, until the curry leaves turn crisp. Remove from heat and pour the hot tempering over the chutney and mix well to combine. Refrigerated, this keeps well for 2 days.

Green Coconut Chutney

Preparation Time
15 mins

Makes
300 gm

Ingredients

1½ Tbsp Bengal gram (chana dal), split
1 cup Grated fresh coconut
½ cup Coriander leaves
2 Small green chillies
½-inch Ginger piece
Salt, to taste
¼ cup Water
1 Tbsp Coconut oil
1 tsp Black mustard seeds
1 tsp Black gram (urad dal), split and skinned
5–8 Curry leaves
1 Dried red chilli
1 tsp Fenugreek seeds

Method

1. Place the chana dal in a pan on low heat and roast for 2–3 minutes. Set aside.
2. Place the coconut, coriander leaves, chana dal, green chillies, ginger, salt and ¼ cup water in a food processor and blitz to a coarse paste. Transfer the paste into a bowl and set aside.
3. Heat the coconut oil in a pan over medium heat. Once the oil is hot, add the mustard seeds and urad dal; sauté for 30–45 seconds.
4. Add in the curry leaves, red chilli and fenugreek seeds, and fry for 30–40 seconds, until the curry leaves turn crisp. Remove from heat and pour the hot tempering over the chutney and mix well to combine. Refrigerated, this keeps well for 2 days.

Aam Ki Launji

Sweet and sour mango chutney

Cooking Time 25 mins

Makes 400 gm

Ingredients

- 2 large Raw mango, peeled
- ½ cup Mustard oil
- 1 tsp Cumin seeds
- 1 tsp Fennel seeds
- ½ tsp Nigella seeds
- ¼ tsp Fenugreek seeds
- ½ tsp Coriander powder
- ½ tsp Turmeric
- 1 tsp Red chilli powder
- Water, as needed
- ¼ cup Jaggery
- Salt, to taste
- 1 tsp Roasted cumin powder

Method

1. Cut the raw mangoes into slices or chunks.
2. Heat the mustard oil in a pan over high heat. Once the oil is smoking, reduce the heat to medium and add the cumin, fennel, nigella and fenugreek seeds and allow them to crackle. This will take 30 seconds.
3. Turn the heat to low, add the coriander, turmeric, chilli powder and 1 Tbsp water and mix well. Fry for 1 minute, until the spices release their aromas.
4. Add the mango and mix well to coat them evenly. Cook for 2–3 minutes.
5. Pour 1 cup water into the pan and mix well. Cook for 5–7 minutes, until the mangoes are softened.
6. Add the jaggery and salt. Simmer until the jaggery is dissolved and the mixture reduces to a sticky consistency.
7. To finish, add roasted cumin powder and stir well. Cook for 2–3 minutes.
8. Cool to room temperature and serve. Refrigerated, this keeps well for 2 weeks.

Mango Chutney

Cooking Time 15 mins

Makes 200 gm

Ingredients

- 2 Ripe mangoes, peeled and deseeded
- 2 Tbsp Cooking oil
- 2 Dried red chillies
- ¼ tsp Black mustard seeds
- Salt, to taste
- Juice from 1 lemon

Method

1. Place half the mango in a food processor and blitz it into a purée. Cut the rest into small cubes.
2. Heat the oil in a pan over medium heat. Add the chillies and mustard seeds. Once the mustard seeds start spluttering, turn the heat to low and add the mangoes.
3. Season with salt and cook for 2 minutes, or until the mangoes are softened slightly.
4. Add the lemon juice and mix well. Remove from heat, let the chutney cool down completely, and transfer to an airtight container. Refrigerated, this keeps well for 10 days.

Green Garlic Chutney

Preparation Time 10 mins

Makes 300 gm

Ingredients

- 30 Sprigs green garlic
- ⅓ cup Coriander leaves
- 5 Green chillies
- Salt to taste
- 2 Tbsp Water
- 1 Tbsp Roasted peanuts or coconut (optional)
- Lemon juice, to taste

Method

1. Roughly chop the garlic, coriander leaves and chillies.
2. Place the chopped ingredients in a food processor with a pinch of salt and water. Blitz it to a smooth paste. If using, add the peanuts or coconut as well.
3. Stir in the lemon juice, taste and add more salt, if required. Store in an airtight container. Refrigerated, this keeps well for a week.

Pudina Dhania Chutney

Mint and Coriander Chutney

Preparation Time 15 mins

Makes 400 gm

Ingredients

- 1½ cup Mint leaves
- 1 cup Coriander leaves
- 1–2 Garlic cloves, peeled
- ½-inch Ginger piece, peeled
- 1 Green chilli
- 1 Tbsp Lime juice
- ¼ tsp Salt
- ¼ tsp Cumin seeds
- ½ tsp Chaat masala
- 1 tsp Sugar
- ¼ cup Chilled water

Method

1. Wash the coriander leaves and mint leaves thoroughly. Dry them using paper towels. Set aside.
2. Place a pan on low heat and add the cumin seeds. Dry roast the seeds for 1–2 minutes, until the cumin turns dark brown and fragrant. Set aside.
3. Place the mint, coriander leaves, garlic, ginger, chilli, lime juice, salt, roasted cumin, chaat masala, sugar and chilled water into a food processor and blitz to a smooth paste.
4. If required, add more water, 1 Tbsp at a time and blend till the chutney reaches a smooth consistency. Check seasoning and adjust as desired. Refrigerated, this chutney keeps well for 2 days.

Lehsun Mirchi Chutney

Garlic and chilli chutney

Preparation Time
10 mins

Makes
130 gm

Ingredients

- 2 Large garlic bulbs, peeled
- 1 Tbsp Red chilli powder
- 1 Tbsp Coriander powder
- ½ tsp Cumin powder
- 2 Tbsp Ghee
- ½ tsp Cumin seeds
- Salt, to taste
- Juice from ½ lemon

Method

1. Add the peeled garlic, red chilli powder, coriander powder and cumin powder in a food processor and blitz into a coarse paste.
2. Heat the ghee on a pan over medium heat. Once the ghee is hot, add the cumin seeds and fry for 30 seconds, until it splutters.
3. Add the garlic-spice paste to the pan and cook for 8–10 minutes, until the raw smell of garlic and spices dissipates.
4. Season with salt and mix well to combine. Remove from heat and allow it to cool to room temperature.
5. Once the chutney is cool, add the lemon juice and mix. Refrigerated, this keeps well for 5 days.

Litchi Mirchi Chutney

Litchi and chilli chutney

Preparation Time
20 mins

Makes
300 gm

Ingredients

- 2 Green chillies
- 500 gm Tinned litchis in syrup, drained
- 2-3 Sprigs coriander
- ¼-inch Ginger piece
- Salt, to taste
- ¼ tsp Black pepper powder
- Juice from 1 lime

Method

1. Char the green chillies by placing them over the heat using tongs, or use a blowtorch and char until the skin of the chilli is scorched black.
2. Once slightly cooled, peel the outer skin off. If you want to avoid spice, deseed the chillies as well.
3. Place the litchis, chillies, coriander and ginger in a food processor and blitz to a chunky purée.
4. Add the salt, pepper and lime juice and mix well. Transfer to an airtight container and store in the fridge. Refrigerated, this keeps well for 3 days.

Tomato Jaggery Chutney

Cooking Time
25 mins

Makes
250 gm

Ingredients

- 100 ml Mustard oil
- ¼ tsp Panch phoran (use black mustard seeds, if not available)
- 2 Dried red chillies
- 4 Medium-sized tomatoes, diced
- ½ -inch Ginger piece, chopped
- ¼ tsp Turmeric
- Juice from ½ lemon
- 3 Tbsp Jaggery
- Salt, to taste

Method

1. Heat the mustard oil in a pan over a high heat, until it smokes. Once the oil is hot, add the panch phoran, dried red chillies and fry for 40 seconds.
2. Add the tomatoes to the pan, along with the ginger and turmeric. Cook over medium heat for 5–6 minutes, or until the tomatoes have softened.
3. Add in the lemon juice and cook for 5 minutes, until the tomatoes are completely mushy.
4. Add the jaggery and bring to a boil. This will take 3 minutes. Turn the heat to low and simmer for 2–3 minutes, or until the chutney has reached a thick syrupy consistency.
5. Remove from heat, let the chutney cool and transfer to an airtight container. Refrigerated, this keeps well for up to 2 weeks.

Doon Chetin

Kashmiri walnut chutney

Preparation Time
15 mins

Makes
600 gm

Ingredients

- 1 cup Walnut kernels (soaked in warm water for 2 hours and peeled)
- 1 Medium-sized onion, sliced
- 10 Mint leaves
- 4 Green chillies
- 2 cups Plain yoghurt (use thick yoghurt preferably)
- ½ tsp Coarsely ground black cumin seeds
- Salt, to taste

Method

1. Place the walnut, onion, mint and green chillies together in a food processor and blitz, till it forms a slightly coarse paste.
2. Place the yoghurt in a bowl and add the cumin, salt, walnut paste. Mix well to combine.
3. Chill for a minimum of 30 minutes before serving. Refrigerated, this will keep well for 2 days.
4. Eaten with non-vegetarian kebabs or rice dishes, traditionally doon chetin is prepared in a mortar and pestle which gives it a slightly coarse texture.

Coriander Salsa

Preparation Time
25 mins

Makes
400 gm

Ingredients

- 1 tsp Cooking oil
- 2 Dried red chillies
- 10–15 Garlic cloves (divided)
- 1 cup Olive oil
- 150 gm Coriander leaves, finely chopped
- Salt, to taste
- ½ tsp Black pepper powder
- Juice from 2 small limes

Method

1. Heat the oil in a pan over medium heat. Add the red chillies and fry for 30 seconds, or until they turn brown and crisp. Set them aside to cool and then chop finely.
2. Take half the garlic and blend into a paste with a little dash of olive oil and finely chop the other half.
3. Place the coriander leaves in a bowl, and add in the garlic paste and the chopped garlic. Add in the fried chopped red chillies.
4. Season with salt, black pepper and lemon juice. Drizzle the rest of the olive oil into the bowl while mixing. Once it is well combined, store in the refrigerator. This keeps well for 3 days.
5. Drizzle on top of grilled fish, vegetables or kebabs for an instant zesty lift.

Raw Mango Salsa

Preparation Time
10 mins

Makes
200 gm

Ingredients

- 2 Raw mangoes, peeled and chopped into small dices
- 2 Green chillies, deseeded and finely chopped
- 2 tsp Sumac powder
- Salt, to taste
- 2 Tbsp Olive oil

Method

1. Add the raw mangoes and green chillies into a bowl. Season with sumac and salt. Drizzle in the olive oil and mix well.
2. Refrigerated, this keeps well for 3 days. Spoon on top of kebabs, grills or cutlets to add a fresh, acidic punch to the dishes.

Burani Raita

Hyderabadi-style spiced yoghurt

Preparation Time 15 mins

Makes 400 gm

Ingredients

- 2 cups Yoghurt
- 6 Garlic cloves, peeled and finely chopped
- ¼ tsp Red chilli powder
- ½ tsp Roasted cumin powder
- Salt, to taste

Method

1. Add the yoghurt to a mixing bowl. Using a whisk or a fork, beat the yoghurt until smooth.
2. Add the garlic, red chilli powder, cumin powder and salt. Mix well to combine. Serve chilled. Refrigerated, this keeps well for 2 days. Serve this with biryanis, kebabs or rolls.

Mint Yoghurt

Preparation Time 10 mins

Makes 250 gm

Ingredients

- ¼ cup Coriander leaves
- ¼ cup Mint leaves
- 1 Green chilli
- 2 Tbsp Water
- 1 cup Yoghurt
- ½ tsp Sugar
- ¼ tsp Roasted cumin powder
- ¼ tsp Garam masala
- Salt, to taste
- Juice from ½ lemon

Method

1. Place coriander, mint leaves, chilli and 2 Tbsp water in a food processor and blitz to a smooth paste.
2. In a bowl, add the yoghurt and mix in the herb paste, sugar, cumin, garam masala, salt, lemon juice and whisk the mixture to combine. Serve chilled. This will keep well for 2–3 days in the refrigerator.
3. Serve this with biryanis, kebabs or rolls.

Beetroot Yoghurt

Cooking Time
55 mins

Makes
200 gm

Ingredients

1–2 Medium-sized beetroot
Salt, to taste
Cooking oil, as needed
1 cup Greek yoghurt
1 tsp Sugar (optional)
1 Tbsp Ghee
¼ tsp Mustard seeds
5–8 Curry leaves
2 Green chilli, slit in half
1 pinch Asafoetida

Method

1. Preheat oven to 180 degrees C.
2. Evenly coat the beetroots with some salt and oil and wrap them individually in aluminium foil. Roast in the oven for 35–40 minutes, or until a skewer can pierce through the flesh easily.
3. Once the beetroots are cool, grate them into thick strips and place in a mixing bowl. Add in the Greek yoghurt, sugar (if using) and salt to taste.
4. Heat the ghee in a pan over medium heat. Once the ghee is hot, add the mustard seeds and curry leaves and stir-fry for 30 seconds, until it splutters. Add in the green chillies, asafoetida and fry for 30–40 seconds.
5. Remove from heat, and pour the tempering over the yoghurt and mix well. Let it cool and serve. Consume the same day.
6. This yoghurt can be served as a side dish or it works just as well as a dip.

Hummus

Preparation Time
30 mins

Makes
1 kg

Ingredients

1½ cups Chickpeas
4½ cups Water
⅓ cup Tahini
2 Tbsp Extra-virgin olive oil
2 Tbsp Fresh lemon juice
1 Garlic clove
½ tsp Salt
5 Tbsp Iced water

Method

1. Soak the chickpeas in 5 cups water, overnight or for a minimum of 8 hours. The water should exceed the amount of legumes, as they will hydrate and double in size. Drain and set aside.
2. Add the drained chickpeas in a pressure cooker, along with 4½ cups water on medium heat. Pressure cook for 4 whistles and remove from heat. Allow the steam to release on its own. Open the pressure cooker lid and drain the chickpeas. Set aside to cool.
3. Place the chickpeas, tahini, olive oil, lemon juice, garlic and salt in a food processor and blitz to a smooth paste. Scrap down the sides of the mixing jar while blending, if necessary. Add more water and blend further if the is still chunky, until it reaches a smooth consistency. Refrigerated, hummus keeps well for 3 days.

Sides

Pickled Baby Onions

Scarlet Kidney Beans and Tomato Salad

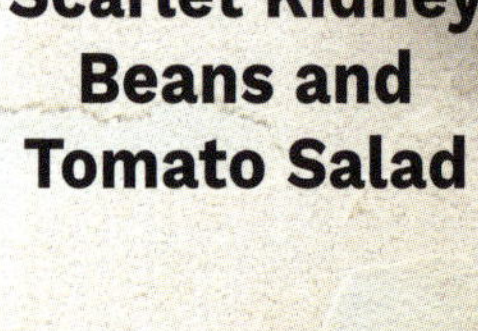

Kachumber

Beetroot Carpaccio

Purple Cabbage and Green Peas Salad

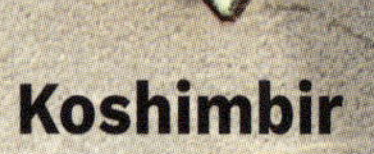

Koshimbir

Pomegranate Salad

Mango and
Rocket Salad
Beans Thoran
Carrot Thoran
Lentil Salad
Cucumber
Thoran
Jeera
Aloo
Kala Chana
Chaat
Masala
Onions

Masala Onions

Preparation Time
20 mins

Serves
4

Ingredients

3 Large onions
Chilled water, as required
Salt, to taste
½ tsp Chaat masala
1 tsp Kashmiri red chilli powder
1 tsp Coriander powder
1–2 tsp Finely chopped coriander leaves
2–3 tsp Lime juice

Method

1. Slice the onions into 2 mm thick roundels. Fill a bowl with chilled water and soak the onions in it for 10–15 minutes. This step reduces the pungency of the onions and turns them crisp. Separate the rings while they are soaking.
2. Drain the water from the onions and pat them dry with a paper towel.
3. Add the salt, chaat masala, red chilli powder, coriander powder, coriander leaves and lime juice. Toss and serve. This needs to be served as soon as it is prepared, as the onions begin to turn soft when they are removed from the cold water.

Pickled Baby Onions

Preparation Time
10 mins

Serves
4

Ingredients

15–20 Shallots (sambar onions), peeled
1 tsp Vinegar or apple cider vinegar
¼ cup Water
¾ tsp Salt

Method

1. Rinse the peeled onions in water and drain them well. Place them in a glass or a ceramic jar, or any other non-reactive vessel.
2. In a bowl, combine the vinegar, water and salt. Add this mixture to the onions. Seal the jar and shake it. Let the onions sit in the vinegar solution for 2–3 days. Shake the bottle 2–3 times a day. Once the onions have pickled, keep the jar refrigerated. These will keep well in the refrigerator for up to 2 weeks.

Quick tip

Regular onions, sliced into rounds can also be used for pickling. The sambar onions lend the pickle its distinctive red colour, add a small piece of beetroot to mimic the colour when using regular onions.

Ginger, chillies, peppercorns can be added to the pickling liquid for additional flavour. When the onions get over, add more to the leftover pickling liquid till all of it is used up.

Koshimbir

Tempered Maharastrian salad

Cooking Time 15 mins

Serves 4

Ingredients

- 4 Tbsp Roasted peanuts
- 2 Cucumbers, finely chopped
- 1 Tbsp Ghee
- 1 tsp Cumin seeds
- 1 pinch Asafoetida
- 1 Green chilli, slit lengthwise
- Salt, to taste
- 1 tsp Sugar
- 1 Tbsp Lemon juice
- 10 sprigs Coriander leaves, finely chopped

Method

1. Roughly crush the peanuts to a coarse consistency in a mortar and pestle or a food processor. Set aside.
2. Place the cucumbers in a large mixing bowl.
3. Heat a small pan on medium heat and add the ghee. Once the ghee is hot, add the cumin seeds and asafoetida. Fry for 45 seconds. Remove from heat and pour the tempering over the chopped cucumbers.
4. Add the ground peanuts, green chilli, salt, sugar, lemon juice and coriander. Mix well and serve immediately.

Purple Cabbage and Green Peas Salad

Cooking Time 20 mins

Serves 4

Ingredients

- 1 cup Green peas
- 6 cups Purple cabbage, thinly sliced
- ¼ cup Olive oil
- ¼ cup Vinegar, or apple cider vinegar
- Salt, to taste
- 1 tsp Honey

Method

1. Place a pot on medium heat, add 2 cups water and bring to a boil. Meanwhile, set up a bowl with ice water.
2. Add the fresh peas to the boiling water. Cover and let the peas simmer for 8–10 minutes. Drain and plunge into the ice water for 1 minute. Remove from the ice water and set aside. If using frozen peas, cover and cook for 3 minutes, then drain and add to the ice water.
3. Place the cabbage and green peas in a mixing bowl.
4. To make the dressing, take a small jar and add the olive oil, vinegar, salt and honey. Shake to combine. Pour the dressing on the salad and toss to coat evenly. Serve immediately.

Kachumber

Zesty chopped salad

Preparation Time 10 mins

Serves 4

Ingredients

⅓	cup	Finely chopped, onions,
½	cup	Finely chopped, tomatoes
½	cup	Finely chopped, cucumbers
½	cup	Sprouts/diced avocados/diced semi-ripe mangoes (optional)
1	Tbsp	Chopped mint leaves
¼	cup	Chopped coriander leaves
½–1	tsp	Chopped green chillies
½	tsp	Roasted cumin powder (p. 11)
¼	tsp	Red chilli powder or cayenne pepper
1–2	tsp	Lemon juice
2		Pinches of salt

Method

1. Combine the onions, tomatoes, cucumbers in a mixing bowl. Depending on the variation of the kachumber salad you would prefer, add in sprouts, avocado or mangoes.
2. Add the mint, coriander leaves, green chillies, cumin and chilli powder, and mix to combine.
3. Add in the lemon juice and salt only when ready to serve, as adding these ingredients will draw out moisture from the vegetables. Mix well and serve immediately.

Pomegranate Salad

Preparation Time 5 mins

Serves 4

Ingredients

2	cups	Pomegranate seeds
1		Medium-sized red onion, thinly sliced
15		Mint leaves, roughly torn
		Juice from 1 lemon
		Salt, to taste
1	tsp	Chaat masala
⅓	cup	Chopped walnuts

Method

1. Add the pomegranate, onion, mint in a mixing bowl.
2. When ready to serve, add in the lemon juice, salt and chaat masala. Mix well to combine. Toss in the walnuts, mix and serve immediately.

Lentil Salad

Cooking Time

50 mins

Serves

4

Ingredients

3⁄ cup Split yellow mung bean (moong dal) or whole black lentils (urad dal)
1 tsp Cooking oil
1⁄ tsp Red chilli powder
1⁄ tsp Turmeric
Salt, to taste
Water, as required
1⁄ cup Grated carrot
1 Tomato, chopped
1⁄ cup Chopped red onion
1⁄ cup Chopped apple
1 Green chilli, chopped
2⁄ -inch Ginger piece, minced
1⁄ cup Chopped coriander leaves
2 Tbsp Chopped mint leaves
2⁄ tsp Chaat masala
2⁄ tsp Cumin powder
1⁄ tsp Paprika
2 tsp Lime juice

Method

1. Wash the yellow lentils thoroughly and soak in water for a minimum of an hour. If using black lentils, wash and soak overnight.
2. To cook the lentils, place a large pan over medium heat and add the oil. Once the oil is hot, add the drained dal and sauté for 5 minutes. Add in the chilli powder, turmeric, ½ tsp salt and 1 cup water and stir to mix. Cover and cook for 6–8 minutes or until all the water has been absorbed and the dal is cooked. For the black lentils, add 2½ cups water and cook for 25–30 minutes, until done.
3. Transfer the cooked dal to a bowl and fluff while it is warm. Add in the carrot, tomato, onion, apple, green chilli, ginger, coriander and mint. Mix to combine.
4. Add the chaat masala, cumin, paprika, lime juice, salt and toss again. Taste and adjust seasoning if required. This salad can also be served cold. Refrigerated, this keeps well for 2 days.

Kala Chana Chaat

Bengal gram chaat

Cooking Time 40 mins

Serves 4

Ingredients

1 cup	Whole Bengal gram (kala chana)
3 cups	Water
⅓ cup	Chopped tomato
⅓ cup	Chopped onion
1–2	Green chillies chopped
1–2 Tbsp	Chopped coriander leaves
1–2 Tbsp	Chopped mint leaves
1 tsp	Chaat masala
¼ tsp	Cumin powder
¼ tsp	Dried mango powder (amchur)
¼ tsp	Red chilli powder
	Salt, to taste
	Juice from 1 lemon

Method

1. Wash the Bengal gram thoroughly and soak them in 4 cups water overnight or for a minimum of 4 hours. Drain the gram and set aside.
2. Place a large pot over medium-high heat. Add in 3 cups water, along with the soaked gram. Cover and boil for 30 minutes, fully submerged in water, until done. Once they are boiled, drain and place the lentils in a large bowl.
3. Add the tomato, onion, green chillies, coriander and mint in the bowl. Add in the chaat masala, cumin, dried mango powder, chilli powder and mix well to combine. Finish with salt and lemon juice. Serve immediately.

Beet Carpaccio

Cooking Time 60 mins

Serves 4

Ingredients

1	Large-sized beetroot, skin on
2 Tbsp	Extra-virgin olive oil
2 Tbsp	Gondhoraj lemon juice
½ Tbsp	Gondhoraj lemon zest
1 tsp	Kasundi (Bengali mustard)
½ tsp	Honey
	Salt, to taste
	Black pepper powder, to taste
1 cup	Rocket leaves
2 Tbsp	Chopped walnuts

Method

1. Preheat oven to 200 degrees C.
2. Wrap the beet tightly in foil, place in an baking dish and roast until the beetroot is cooked. This can take around 45 minutes–1 hour 15 minutes. Once the beet is cooked, remove from the oven and set aside to cool. The baked beet can be stored wrapped in the foil in the fridge for 3–4 days.
3. Peel the beet. Use a mandolin, and slice it into wafer-thin slices. Beets can stain, so wear gloves and use a plate that doesn't stain.
4. To make the dressing, add the olive oil, lemon juice, zest, kasundi, honey in a small bowl and whisk them together to emulsify.
5. Place the rocket leaves in a small bowl, add half of the vinaigrette and mix well. Take another plate and arrange the beet slices so that they are slightly overlapping, place the rocket leaves on one side of the plate. Sprinkle the chopped walnuts over it, drizzle the rest of the vinaigrette over the salad and serve.

Rocket and Candy Cane Beetroot Salad

Preparation Time 10 mins

Serves 4

Ingredients

- 1 Medium-sized candy cane beet
- 3 cups Rocket leaves
- ¼ cup Fresh orange juice
- 2 Tbsp Balsamic vinegar
- 1 Tbsp Dijon mustard
- 2 tsp Honey
- Black pepper powder, to taste

Method

1. Peel the beet. Use a mandolin and make thin, round slices of the beet. Try to slice them in complete circles as much as possible, but don't fret over it if the slices are not perfect.
2. Place the rocket leaves in the bowl and top with the beet slices.
3. Add the orange juice, vinegar, mustard, honey and pepper in a small bowl and whisk together to combine. Alternatively, add these ingredients in a small jar with a tight lid and shake to mix well. Drizzle over the salad and serve.

Scarlet Kidney Beans and Tomato Salad

Cooking Time 40 mins

Serves 4

Ingredients

- 2 cups Scarlet kidney beans
- 5 cups Water
- 1 Onion, thinly sliced
- 2 Tbsp Red wine vinegar
- 2 cups Sweet cherry tomatoes
- 1 tsp Fine sea salt
- 2 Tbsp Extra-virgin olive oil

Method

1. Soak the kidney beans in 6 cups water for 8 hours. Drain and set aside.
2. Place a pressure cooker on medium heat and add the beans to it along with 5 cups water. Secure the pressure cooker lid and cook for 4–5 whistles. Turn off the heat, and allow the steam to release naturally. This will take 15 minutes. The beans should be tender and cooked through completely. Drain the excess water, and set the beans aside to cool to room temperature.
3. In a small bowl, combine onions and vinegar and set aside for 10–15 minutes.
4. Halve the cherry tomatoes and place in a serving bowl. Sprinkle with 1 tsp salt. Add the kidney beans and onions along with the vinegar and olive oil. Toss gently to mix and serve.

Mango and Rocket Salad

Cooking Time

15 mins

Serves

4

Ingredients

- ¼ cup Lemon juice
- 2 Garlic cloves, grated
- 1 tsp Dijon mustard
- ¼ tsp Salt
- ¼ tsp Black pepper powder
- ½ tsp Honey
- ⅓ cup Extra-virgin olive oil
- 6 cups Rocket leaves
- 2 cups Ripe, but firm mango, peeled and chopped into bite-sized pieces
- 20 Pitted cherries
- 1 Tbsp Chopped almonds
- 2 Tbsp Amaranth pops

Method

1. To make the vinaigrette, combine the lemon juice, garlic, mustard, salt, pepper and honey in a bowl. Drizzle in the olive oil while whisking the rest of the ingredients, until the dressing emulsifies.
2. Alternatively, combine everything in a jar with a tight lid and shake to combine. Refrigerated, this dressing keeps well for 1 week.
3. Add the rocket leaves, mango, cherries and almonds in a bowl. Pour in the dressing and gently toss to coat the salad evenly. Sprinkle the amaranth pops over the salad and serve immediately.

Variation

Add 1 cup boiled white kidney beans and 10 carrom (ajwain) leaves in step 2 of the recipe to make a white kidney bean, mango and rocket salad. To cook the beans, soak them in water for 8 hours. Drain and add them to a pressure cooker, along with 3 cups water and cook on medium heat for 4–5 whistles. Let the steam release on its own, then drain the water. Allow the beans to cool to room temperature, then add it to the salad.

Thoran

Coconut-infused vegetable preparation

Cooking Time
20 mins

Serves
4

Ingredients

- 1 Tbsp Coconut oil
- ½ tsp Mustard seeds
- ½ tsp Cumin seeds
- 6–7 Shallots (sambar onions), halved/¼–⅓ cup chopped onions
- 3–4 Garlic cloves, finely chopped
- 1 Green chilli, chopped
- 10–11 Curry leaves
- ¼ tsp Turmeric
- 1½ cup Chopped french beans/grated carrot
- ½ cup Grated fresh or frozen coconut
- Salt, to taste
- 2 Tbsp Water

Method

1. Heat the coconut oil in a heavy, deep-bottomed pan on low heat. Once the oil is hot, add the mustard and cumin seeds, and fry for 30 seconds.
2. Add the onions and sauté for 2 minutes, until translucent. Add the garlic, green chilli, curry leaves and sauté on low heat for 1 minute till the garlic softens. Add the turmeric and sauté for 30 seconds.
3. Add the beans/carrot and sauté for 1 minute. Add the coconut, salt and sauté for 2 minutes. Add 2 Tbsp water and cook for 1 minute. Now cover the pan with a lid and cook on low heat for 3–4 minutes. If using carrots, remove from heat.
4. If using beans, check to see if they are done. If water has dried up and the beans are uncooked, add 1 Tbsp water and stir. Cover and cook till the beans are tender. If there is water left in the pan after the beans are done, then cook uncovered until the water evaporates. Refrigerated, this keeps well for 3 days.

Cucumber Thoran

Cooking Time
10 mins

Serves
4

Ingredients

- 1½ Tbsp Coconut oil
- 1 Tbsp Mustard seeds
- 1 Green chilli, chopped
- 1 sprig Curry leaves
- 1 pinch Asafoetida
- ¼ tsp Turmeric
- 2 Cucumbers, peeled and cut into 1-inch dices
- 2 Tbsp Grated fresh or frozen coconut
- Salt, to taste

Method

1. Heat the coconut oil in a heavy, deep-bottomed pan over medium heat. Once the oil is hot, add the mustard seeds and let them splutter for 15–20 seconds.
2. Add the green chilli, curry leaves, asafoetida and turmeric. Sauté for 1 minute on medium heat, until the curry leaves crisp up.
3. Add the cucumber and sauté for 2–3 minutes on medium heat. Add the coconut, salt and stir-fry for a 1 minute. Remove from heat and serve.

Kurkuri Bhindi

Mustard Baby Potatoes

Rocket and Candy Cane Beetroot Salad

Khatta Meetha Kaddu

Pyaaz Aloo Bhajiya

Sesame Snow Peas

Luchi

Nimbu Mirchi Broccoli

Saag

Mirchi Ka Salan

Jhatpat Aloo

Pyaaz Aloo Bhajiya

Onion and potato fritters

Cooking Time

30 mins

Serves

4

Ingredients

1½ cup	Red onions, thinly sliced
	Salt, to taste
1½ cup	Grated potatoes
2	Green chillies, chopped
3	Garlic cloves, minced
½ tsp	Cumin powder
1 tsp	Red chilli powder
½ tsp	Turmeric
½ tsp	Coriander powder
½ cup	Gram flour (besan)
2–3 Tbsp	Rice flour
2 cups	Cooking oil for frying

Method

1. Place the onion slices in a bowl and sprinkle 1 tsp salt over it and massage it in well – this helps draw out the moisture, and make the fritters crispy. Let it rest for 15 minutes, then squeeze out the water from the onions and set aside in a mixing bowl.
2. Meanwhile, soak the grated potatoes in cold water for 15 minutes, to remove excess starch. Drain and squeeze out the excess water and add it to the drained onions.
3. Add in the green chillies, garlic, cumin, chilli powder, turmeric, coriander powder, gram flour and rice flour. Use your hands to mix the ingredients well, to form a batter. The water in the vegetables will form a tight but moist mix; if the mix looks dry add in 2 Tbsp water. While adding water, stop before the mix turns soggy, as that will prevent the fritters from turning crispy.
4. Heat the oil in a frying pan on medium heat. To test if the oil is ready for frying, drop a bit of the batter into it – if it bubbles and rises up immediately, then it's ready. Meanwhile, set up a plate lined with paper towels.
5. Once the oil is hot, use a spoon, or use your hands and take rough amounts of the fritter mix – they don't have to be uniform or shaped any particular way – and drop them carefully in the oil. Fry these fritters for 5–7 minutes, until they are golden brown. Carefully take them out of the oil with a slotted spoon and place them on the paper towel-lined plate. Serve hot.

Kurkuri Bhindi

Crispy-fried okra

Cooking Time

45 mins

Serves

4

Ingredients

- 500 gm Okra
- ½ tsp Turmeric
- 1 tsp Red chilli powder or paprika
- 1 tsp Coriander powder
- 1 tsp Cumin powder
- 1 tsp Dried mango powder (amchur)
- 1 tsp Chaat masala, extra for garnish
- Salt, to taste
- ½ cup Gram flour (besan)
- 2 cups Cooking oil, for frying

Method

1. Rinse the okra in water 3–4 times. Wipe them completely dry with a paper towel. Trim off the crown and the tip. Slice each okra vertically into 4 pieces.
2. Place the sliced okra in a bowl and sprinkle in the turmeric, chilli, coriander, cumin, dried mango powder, chaat masala and salt. Gently mix to combine.
3. In the same bowl, add in the gram flour and gently mix to ensure that it evenly coats the okra slices. Set aside to marinate for 20–30 minutes. Meanwhile, set up a plate lined with paper towels.
4. Heat the oil in a frying pan on medium heat. Once the oil is hot, add the marinated okra in batches and fry, stirring continuously for 5 minutes, until they turn golden brown and crisp.
5. Using a slotted spoon, remove the fried okra on the paper towel-lined plate to drain the extra oil. Sprinkle chaat masala on the crispy fried okra before serving.

Variation

To skip frying the okra, spread the marinated okra in a greased tray. Brush 1 Tbsp oil on the top of the okra, or add 1 Tbsp oil in step 3 and mix well. Bake in a preheated oven at 180 degrees C for 18–20 minutes, until the okra are crisp and golden.

Khatta Meetha Kaddu

Sweet and sour pumpkin

Cooking Time

30 mins

Serves

4

Ingredients

- 40 gm Tamarind
- 1 cup Water (divided), ⅟ cup hot and ½ cup at room temperature
- 2 Tbsp Mustard oil
- 2 tsp Fenugreek seeds
- 2 Dried red chillies
- 250 gm Pumpkin, cut into 1-inch pieces
- Salt, to taste
- ⅟ tsp Turmeric
- 1 tsp Red chilli powder
- 2 Tbsp Jaggery powder

Method

1. To make tamarind water, soak the tamarind in ½ cup hot water in a bowl for 15 minutes. When the water turns cool, mash the tamarind with your hands and remove the shell and veins. Set a mesh strainer over a clean bowl, and pour this liquid through it. Using a spoon, push out as much liquid and pulp as possible. Discard the remains from the strainer.
2. To make the pumpkin, heat the mustard oil in a heavy-bottomed pan over high heat till it is smoking. Turn the heat to low, add the fenugreek seeds and sauté for 20 seconds. Add the red chillies and sauté for 30 seconds.
3. Add the pumpkin, along with the salt, turmeric, chilli powder and sauté for 1 minute on medium heat. Cover the pan and cook for 5 minutes.
4. Add 4 Tbsp tamarind water, jaggery and ⅟ cup water. Cover and cook for 5 minutes. Serve warm. Refrigerated this keeps well for 4 days.

Mirchi Ka Salan

Curried chilli peppers

Cooking Time

30 mins

Serves

4

Ingredients

- 5 Tbsp Coconut or peanut oil (divided)
- 5 Medium-sized onions, sliced
- 10 Tbsp Peanuts
- 5 Tbsp Sesame seeds
- 5 Tbsp Coriander seeds
- 5 Tbsp Cumin seeds (divided)
- 2 sprigs Curry leaves
- ½ tsp Fenugreek seeds
- 1 tsp Black mustard seeds
- 1 Tbsp Ginger-garlic paste (p. 9)
- 2 tsp Red chilli powder
- ½ tsp Turmeric
- 2 cups Grated fresh coconut
- ½ kg Large green chillies, slit and deseeded
- 2 Tbsp Tamarind pulp
- Salt, to taste

Method

1. Heat 2 Tbsp oil in a pan over medium heat. Once the oil is hot, add the onions in batches and fry for 6–8 minutes, until they turn brown. Set aside to cool, and then grind to a smooth paste.
2. Heat a heavy-bottomed, wide pan on low heat. Add the peanuts to the pan and dry roast for 2–3 minutes, until they are crunchy. Set aside.
3. In the same pan, now add the sesame seeds and dry roast on low heat for 1 minute, until they turn light brown. Set aside.
4. In the same pan, add the coriander seeds, 4½ Tbsp cumin seeds and dry roast on low heat for 1–2 minutes, until the mix turns toasty and fragrant. Add this mix, along with the roasted peanuts and sesame to a food processor and blitz to make a grainy paste.
5. In another pan on high heat, add the remaining oil. Once the oil is hot, turn the heat to medium and add ½ Tbsp cumin seeds, curry leaves, fenugreek seeds, mustard seeds and sauté for 30 seconds, until the curry leaves turn crisp.
6. Add the ginger-garlic paste and sauté for 1 minute. Add the chilli powder and turmeric; give it a quick mix and add 1 Tbsp water.
7. Add the coconut, the peanut-sesame paste, green chillies and cook on low heat for 4–5 minutes, until the chillies soften. Add the tamarind pulp, salt and bring to a boil, then remove from heat. Serve hot. Refrigerated, this keeps well for 3–4 days.

Jeera Aloo

Cumin potatoes

Cooking Time

30 mins

Serves

4

Ingredients

- 2 Medium-sized potatoes, halved
- 1½ Tbsp Cooking oil
- 1½ tsp Cumin seeds
- 1 tsp Finely chopped ginger
- 2 Green chillies, chopped
- ½ tsp Turmeric
- Salt, to taste
- ½ tsp Red chilli powder
- ½ tsp Coriander powder
- 2–3 tsp Lime juice
- 2 Tbsp Chopped coriander leaves

Method

1. To boil the potatoes, place them in a pot, along with 6 cups water and bring to a boil on high heat. Reduce the heat and simmer until the potatoes are tender. This will take 12–18 minutes. Remove from heat and set aside. Or add the potatoes to a pressure cooker along with 4 cups water and cook for 3 whistles. Let the steam release on its own.
2. Drain the potatoes and allow them to cool. Peel and cube them.
3. Heat the oil in a pan on medium heat. Once the oil is hot, add the cumin seeds and sauté for 30 seconds, until they crackle. Add the ginger, green chillies and sauté for 30–40 seconds. Then add the turmeric and cook for 30 seconds.
4. Add the cubed potatoes, salt, red chilli powder and coriander powder. Mix well to evenly coat the potatoes and cook for 1–2 minutes. If the potatoes stick to the pan, add a splash of water and continue to cook for 3–4 minutes.
5. Add in the lime juice and give the potatoes a quick mix. Remove from heat and garnish with chopped coriander. Serve hot.

Mustard Baby Potatoes

Cooking Time
25 mins

Serves
4

Ingredients

500 gm Baby potatoes, skin on
1 Tbsp Cooking oil
1 pinch Asafoetida
1 Tbsp Black mustard seeds
Salt, to taste
1 cup Water
½ tsp Dried mango powder (amchur)
2–3 tsp Lemon juice

Method

1. Wash and scrub potatoes thoroughly. Slightly squash each potato with a cooking hammer or a pestle.
2. Heat the oil in a wide pan or a wok on medium heat. Once the oil is hot, add the asafoetida, mustard seeds and sauté for 30 seconds, or until the mustard seeds start to splutter.
3. Add the potatoes and sauté for 2 minutes. Sprinkle in the salt and add 1 cup water. Stir, then cover and cook on medium-low heat for 15 minutes.
4. Add the dried mango powder, then cover and cook for 5 minutes, until the potatoes are cooked through. Remove from heat and drizzle with the lemon juice before serving. Refrigerated, this will keep well for 4 days.

Jhatpat Aloo

Quick-fix potatoes

Cooking Time
25 mins

Serves
4

Ingredients

2 Medium-sized purple potatoes or regular potatoes
Salt, to taste
2 Tbsp Chopped coriander leaves
½ tsp Chaat masala
½ tsp Lemon juice
¼ tsp Black pepper powder
¼ tsp Red chilli flakes

Method

1. Wash and scrub the potatoes. Cut them in quarters and place in a pot of water with salt and bring to a boil on high heat. Reduce the heat and simmer until the potatoes are fork tender. This will take 10–15 minutes. Or add the potatoes to a pressure cooker along with 4 cups water and cook for 2 whistles.
2. Drain the potatoes, peel them and add to a mixing bowl. Toss in the coriander leaves, chaat masala, lemon juice, black pepper and chilli flakes. Mix well to combine. Serve warm.

Sesame Snow Peas

Cooking Time
12 mins

Serves
4

Ingredients

1 Tbsp	Sesame oil
500 gm	Fresh snow peas, washed and patted dry
3 Tbsp	Lemon juice
	Salt, to taste
	Black pepper powder, to taste
2 tsp	Sesame seeds, for garnish

Method

1. Heat the sesame oil in a large wok, on high heat, until it starts smoking. Turn the heat to low, and add the snow peas.
2. Sauté for 2 minutes and remove from heat.
3. Add the lemon juice, then cover and set aside to rest for 5 minutes. Toss with salt, black pepper, sesame seeds and serve. Store in an airtight container and refrigerate. This keeps well for 4 days.

Variation

To make sesame cow pea beans, prep the beans by cutting each bean into half. In step 2, sauté the beans for 5–7 minutes and remove from heat. Add the lemon juice, cover and set aside to rest for 5 minutes. Add the salt, black pepper, sesame seeds and serve.

Nimbu Mirchi Broccoli

Lime and chilli broccoli

Cooking Time
10 mins

Serves
4

Ingredients

1 cup	Broccoli florets
	Water, as required
1 Tbsp	Unsalted butter
½ Tbsp	Finely chopped green chilli
1 Tbsp	Lemon juice
1 tsp	Grated lemon zest
	Salt, to taste
¼ tsp	Black pepper powder

Method

1. Over high heat, bring a pan of water to a boil. Add the broccoli to the pan, cover and cook for 3 minutes, until tender. Meanwhile, prep a bowl with ice water. Once the florets are done, strain and plunge them into the ice water and let it rest for 1 minute. Once the broccoli is cool, drain well.
2. In a large skillet, melt the butter on medium heat. Once the butter has melted, add the chilli and broccoli and give it a good toss. Cook for 2 minutes.
3. Add the lemon juice and cook for 1 minute on medium heat. Sprinkle in the lemon zest, salt and black pepper. Remove from heat and serve hot. Refrigerated, this will keep well for 2 days.

Saag

Indian-style greens

Cooking Time 35 mins

Serves 4

Ingredients

- 2 litres Water
- ⅓ cup Mustard oil
- Salt, to taste
- ½ tsp Baking soda
- 4 Dried Kashmiri red chillies
- 1 pinch Asafoetida
- 500 gm Collard greens/Malabar spinach/Amaranth leaves, kept whole

Method

1. Add 2 litres water to a large saucepan, place over high heat and bring to a boil. Turn the heat to low and add salt, baking soda, chillies and asafoetida; stir till completely dissolved.
2. Add the greens of your choice to the saucepan and press down with a spatula or large spoon. Bring the water back to a boil and continue to press down with a spatula.
3. Continue cooking the greens on medium heat, stirring occasionally so that they remain submerged. Cook for 20 minutes, until the greens are tender. Remove from heat.
4. Transfer to a serving bowl along with the remaining cooking liquid. Refrigerated, this keeps well for 3 days.

Luchi

Fried flatbread

Cooking Time 50 mins

Serves 4

Ingredients

- 2 cups All-purpose flour (maida)
- ¾ tsp Salt
- 2 tsp Sugar
- 1 Tbsp Ghee/cooking oil
- 100 ml Hot water
- Cooking oil for deep-frying, as required

Method

1. Add the all-purpose flour along with salt, sugar and 1 Tbsp oil/ghee in a mixing bowl. Work in the oil evenly so that a fistful of flour when pressed together retains its shape. Add the hot water and knead the flour for 12 minutes. Cover and rest the dough for 20 minutes.
2. Divide the dough into 18–20 equal portions and set aside to rest for a minimum of 10 minutes. Meanwhile, set up a plate lined with paper towels.
3. Heat the oil in a pan or wok for deep-frying on medium heat. Using a rolling pin, roll the dough into flat discs.
4. Add the rolled luchis into hot oil. Press down gently and rotate to help it puff. This will take 2 minutes. Flip, and fry the other side. Strain using a slotted spoon and place on the paper towel-lined plate to soak up the excess oil. Serve hot.

Grains

Steamed
Rice
Manipuri
Black Rice
Khichdi with
Garlic Tadka
Tamarind
Millet
Barley with
Coconut, Cashew
and Figs

Peas
Pulao
Buttered
Govindobhog
Rice
Kheti Polenta
Tomato
Quinoa
Millet
Tabbouleh

Rice

Cooking Time
25 mins

Serves
4

Ingredients

1½ cups Water
1 cup Basmati rice/sella rice (washed and soaked for 1 hour)

Method

1. Strain the rice.
2. Place the water in a pot and bring it to a boil over medium-high heat. Reduce the heat to low and add the soaked rice. Cover the pot with a lid and cook for 15–18 minutes, or until all the water is absorbed.
3. Turn off the heat and remove the pot from the stove. Keep the lid on and allow to steam for 5 minutes. Serve hot. Refrigerated, this keeps well for 4 days.

Brown Rice

Cooking Time
50 mins

Serves
4

Ingredients

1 cup Brown rice
2 cups Water
2 Tbsp Butter

Method

1. Rinse and strain the rice.
2. Combine the rinsed rice and water in a pot and bring to a boil over medium-high heat. Cover the pot with a lid and reduce the heat to low. Simmer for 45 minutes, or until all the water is absorbed.
3. Remove from heat and let it sit covered for 5 more minutes. Fluff with a fork. Serve hot. Refrigerated, this keeps well for 3–4 days.

Manipuri Black Rice

Cooking Time
40 mins

Serves
4

Ingredients

- 2 Tbsp Butter
- 1 cup Black sticky rice
- 1¾ cups Water

Method

1. Rinse and strain the rice.
2. Heat the butter in a saucepan over medium heat.
3. Once the butter has melted, add the black rice and sauté for 8–10 minutes, until lightly toasted. Take care to stir the rice often, so that it doesn't catch at the bottom of the pan.
4. Add the water and bring to a boil over medium-high heat. Then lower the heat, cover the saucepan with a lid and cook for 25–30 minutes, until the rice is tender and all the water is absorbed. Serve hot. Refrigerated, this keeps well for 3 days.

Buttered Govindobhog Rice

Cooking Time
20 mins

Serves
4

Ingredients

- 1 cup Govindobhog rice
- 2 cups Water
- 2 Tbsp Butter

Method

1. Rinse and strain the rice.
2. Combine the rinsed rice and water in a pot and bring to a boil over medium-high heat. Cover the pot with a lid, reduce the heat to low and simmer for 10–15 minutes, or until all the water is absorbed.
3. Remove from heat and let it sit covered for 5 minutes. Fluff with a fork. Add a big dollop of butter, and serve hot. Refrigerated, this keeps well for 3 days.

Saffron Pilaf

Cooking Time
15 mins

Serves
4

Ingredients

1 gm Saffron
2 Tbsp Hot milk
3 Tbsp Ghee
2 Tbsp Almond slivers
2 cups Cooked white rice (p. 50)
Salt, to taste

Method

1. Gently grind the saffron strands in a mortar and pestle, and add it to the hot milk in a bowl. This step allows the saffron's hue and flavour to fully develop. Set aside.
2. Place the ghee in a pan, over medium heat. Once the ghee is hot, add the almonds followed by the saffron milk. Stir well for 2 minutes on medium heat.
3. Add the rice, salt and mix well for 3–4 minutes. Remove from heat and serve warm. Refrigerated this keeps well for 3 days.

Cumin Rice

Cooking Time
10 mins

Serves
4

Ingredients

2 cups Cooked white rice (p. 50)
3 Tbsp Ghee
1½ Tbsp Cumin seeds
2 Bay leaves
1 One-inch cinnamon stick
2 Star anise
1 Mace
Salt, to taste
1 Tbsp Chopped coriander leaves

Method

1. Place the cooked basmati rice in a large bowl. The rice should be steaming hot.
2. Add the ghee in a pan over medium heat. Once the ghee is hot, add the cumin, bay leaves, cinnamon, star anise and mace. Sauté for 1 minute, until the whole spices turn fragrant.
3. Pour the hot ghee along with the spices to the rice. Season to taste with salt and mix well to combine. Finish with chopped coriander leaves. Remove from heat and serve hot. Refrigerated this keeps well for 2 days.

Peas Pulao

Cooking Time
15 mins

Serves
4

Ingredients

3 Tbsp Ghee
2 Bay leaves
1 One-inch cinnamon stick
2 Black cardamom pods
5 Green cardamom pods
1 Mace
2 Medium-sized onions, finely sliced
1¼ cup Frozen/fresh green peas
1 cup Water, if needed
2 cups Cooked white rice (p. 50)
Salt, to taste

Method

1. Place the ghee in a pan, over medium heat. Once the ghee is hot, add the bay leaves, cinnamon, black and green cardamom pods and mace. Sauté for 1 minute, until the spices turn fragrant.
2. Add the onions and cook for 4–5 minutes, or until they caramelize and turn golden brown.
3. Add the peas, mix and cook for 2–3 minutes, until they are soft. If using fresh green peas, add 1 cup water and cook the peas for 5–6 minutes until soft.
4. Add in the cooked white rice and salt. Mix well to combine. Remove from heat and serve hot. Refrigerated this keeps well for 3 days.

Kabuli Pulao

Cooking Time
40 mins

Serves
4

Ingredients

1 cup Chickpeas, soaked in water
6½ cups Water
3 Tbsp Ghee
2 Bay leaves
1 One-inch cinnamon stick
2 Black cardamom pods
5 Green cardamom pods
1 Mace
2 Medium-sized onions, finely sliced
2 tsp Garam masala
2 cups Cooked white rice (p. 50)
Salt, to taste
2 Tbsp Chopped coriander leaves

Method

1. Soak the chickpeas in water overnight, or for a minimum of 8 hours. Place the chickpeas in a pressure cooker with 6½ cups water on medium heat. Secure the lid and pressure cook on high heat for 3–4 whistles. Turn off the heat and wait for the steam to release from the pressure cooker naturally. Open the lid and drain the chickpeas. The chickpeas should be tender. Set aside.
2. Place the ghee in a pan, over medium heat. Once the ghee is hot, add the bay leaves, cinnamon, cardamon pods and mace. Sauté for 1 minute, until the spices turn fragrant.
3. Add the onions and cook for 3–4 minutes, or until they turn golden brown in colour.
4. Add the garam masala, followed by the cooked chickpeas. Toss and mix well.
5. Add the cooked rice and salt. Cook for 4–5 minutes. Finish with chopped coriander leaves and remove from heat. Refrigerated this keeps well for 3 days.

Tomato Quinoa

Cooking Time

40 mins

Serves

4

Ingredients

- ½ cup Quinoa
- 1 tsp + 1 Tbsp Cooking oil
- 1 cup Water
- 1 ½-inch cinnamon stick
- 1 Green chilli, slit lengthwise
- ½ tsp Cumin seeds
- 8 Garlic cloves, chopped
- ½ cup Chopped onion
- 4 Tomatoes, chopped
- 1 Tbsp Chopped coriander leaves
- Salt, to taste

Method

1. Rinse the quinoa in a bowl and drain. Place a pan on medium heat and add 1 tsp oil. Once the oil is hot, add the drained quinoa and toast for 1 minute.
2. Add 1 cup water and cover the pan with a lid. Cook for 15–20 minutes on medium heat. After 15 minutes, check if the quinoa has absorbed all the water. If there is still water left, cook covered for 5 minutes. Once the water has dried up completely, remove from heat. Set aside for 10 minutes. Then uncover and fluff it up with a fork.
3. Heat 1 Tbsp oil in a pan on medium heat. Add the cinnamon, green chilli, cumin seeds and garlic; and fry for 1 minute.
4. Add the onion and sauté for 2 minutes until transparent. Turn the heat to low, and add the chopped tomatoes and sauté for 4–5 minutes, until mushy.
5. Add the cooked quinoa, coriander and salt. Mix well to combine, then remove from heat. Refrigerated, this keeps well for 3 days.

Khichdi with Garlic Tadka

Cooking Time

35 mins

Serves

4

Ingredients

- 1 cup Split yellow mung bean (moong dal)
- 1 cup Rice
- 4 Tbsp Ghee (divided)
- 2 tsp Cumin seeds
- 1 Small to medium-sized onion, chopped
- 1 Medium-sized tomato, chopped
- 1 tsp Chopped green chillies
- 2 tsp Finely chopped ginger
- ½ tsp Turmeric
- 2 pinch Asafoetida
- Water, as required
- Salt, to taste
- 5–6 Garlic cloves, smashed
- ½ tsp Mustard seeds
- 10–12 Curry leaves

Method

1. Combine the lentils and rice together. Rinse and wash the mix till the water runs clear. Soak the mix for 30 minutes in water. Drain the water and set aside.
2. Heat 2 Tbsp ghee in a pressure cooker over medium heat. Once the ghee is hot, add the cumin seeds. When cumin splutters, add the onions and sauté for 2 minutes, until translucent.
3. Add the tomato, green chilli and ginger and fry for 3 minutes.
4. Add the turmeric and asafoetida, sauté for 3–4 minutes until the tomatoes soften. Add a pinch of salt in this step, as this will make the tomatoes release water ensuring that they don't burn, and speeding up the cooking process.
5. Add the lentil-rice mix to the pressure cooker. Mix well and sauté for a minute. Add 2 cups water and season with salt. Secure the lid and pressure cook on high heat for 4–5 whistles. Turn off the heat, and wait for the steam to release from the pressure cooker naturally.
6. If using a pan to cook the khichdi, pick a deep bottomed one. In step 5, add 4 cups water and stir at regular intervals. Then cover and cook on low-medium heat for 20–25 minutes.
7. Remove the lid and check the consistency. If the khichdi looks too thick, add some hot water and mix well to incorporate. Add more water, if you would like the khichdi to be runnier. Place on low heat and simmer for a few minutes until you get the right consistency.
8. In a small tadka or tempering pan, heat 2 Tbsp ghee on medium heat. Once the ghee is hot, add the garlic and stir-fry for 2 minutes, until light brown. Add the mustard seeds and curry leaves, and sauté for 1 minute, until the curry leaves turn crisp. Pour the temper over the khichdi and mix well. Remove from heat and serve hot.

Millet

Cooking Time
30 mins

Serves
4

Ingredients

1 cup Kodo millet
2¼ cup Water (or vegetable/chicken broth)

Method

1. Place the millet in a sieve and rinse well with cool water.
2. Toasting the millet is optional, but recommended as it lends a deep flavour to the finished dish. For this step, place the rinsed millet in a wide-bottomed saucepan over medium heat. Toast the grains for about 4 minutes, stirring occasionally until the millet turns golden brown and smells fragrant.
3. If you skip step 2, place the millet in a wide-bottomed saucepan over medium heat. Now add the water or broth. Give it a good stir and turn the heat up to high. Bring the mixture to a boil, then lower the heat so the liquid stays at a simmer. Cover the saucepan with a lid and cook for about 15 minutes, or until most of the liquid has been absorbed.
4. Remove from heat and let it sit, with the cover still on, for 10 more minutes. Remove the cover and fluff the millet with a fork. Serve hot. Refrigerated this keeps well for 4–5 days.

Millet Tabbouleh

Cooking Time
10 mins

Serves
4

Ingredients

2 cups Cooked millet, cooled to room temperature (recipe on the left)
½ cup Finely chopped cucumbers
½ cup Finely chopped tomatoes
½ cup Finely chopped red and yellow bell peppers
⅓ cup Finely chopped mint
⅓ cup Finely chopped parsley
⅓ cup Finely chopped spring onions
4 Garlic cloves, finely chopped
Juice from 1½ lemon
1½ Tbsp Olive oil
Black pepper powder, to taste
Salt, to taste
Sugar, to taste

Method

1. In a large mixing bowl, combine the cooked millet with the chopped cucumbers, tomatoes and peppers. Mix well to combine the millet and vegetables.
2. Add in the mint, parsley, spring onions and garlic. Add the lemon juice, olive oil and season with pepper, salt and sugar as per taste. Mix well.
3. Add more lemon juice if you would like it to be tarter. Refrigerated, this keeps well for 3 days.

Ghee and Chilli Millet

Cooking Time
10 mins

Serves
4

Ingredients

- 2 Tbsp Ghee
- 2 tsp Mustard seeds
- 3 Green chillies, finely sliced
- 6 sprigs Coriander leaves, finely chopped
- 2 cups Cooked millet, cooled to room temperature (recipe on facing page)
- Salt, to taste

Method

1. Heat the ghee in a pan over medium heat. Once the ghee is hot, add the mustard seeds and stir for 15 seconds, until they stop spluttering. Add the chillies and coriander and fry for 30 seconds.
2. Add the millet, salt and mix well. Cook for 5 minutes, and remove from heat. Serve warm. Refrigerated, this keeps well for 3 days.

Coconut Millet

Cooking Time
10 mins

Serves
4

Ingredients

- 2 Tbsp Ghee
- 2 tsp Mustard seeds
- 3 Dried red chillies
- 8–10 Curry leaves
- 1 cup Grated coconut
- 2 cups Cooked millet, cooled to room temperature (recipe on facing page)
- Salt, to taste

Method

1. Heat the ghee in a pan over medium heat. Once the ghee is hot, add the mustard seeds and stir for 15 seconds, until they stop spluttering.
2. Add the dry red chillies, curry leaves and grated coconut. Cook for 5 minutes, till the coconut turns light brown in colour.
3. Add in the millet, salt and mix well. Cook for 5–7 minutes and remove from heat. Serve warm. Refrigerated, this keeps well for 3 days.

Coconut Millet
Saffron Pilaf
Tomato Barley
Upma
Brown Rice

Sol Kadhi
Khichdi
Cumin Rice
Poha
Kabuli Pulao
Ghee and
Chilli Millet

Tamarind Millet

Cooking Time
10 mins

Serves
4

Ingredients

6 Tbsp Tamarind paste
2 tsp Turmeric, optional
2 cup Cooked millet, cooled to room temperature (p. 56)
2 Tbsp Sesame oil
2 tsp Mustard seeds
¼ tsp Asafoetida
3 tsp Split Bengal gram (chana dal)
6 Dried red chillies, broken
8–10 Curry leaves
Salt, to taste

Method

1. Take tamarind paste in a small bowl, add 1–2 Tbsp water, turmeric (if using) and mix well to combine.
2. In a large bowl, place the cooked millet. Add the tamarind paste mix and combine well. Set aside.
3. Heat a pan with sesame oil over medium heat. Add the mustard seeds and let it splutter.
4. Add the asafoetida, chana dal and red chillies. Fry for 15 seconds, until the dal turns light brown in colour.
5. Add the curry leaves and fry for 15–20 seconds, until the leaves turn crisp.
6. Add the millet, salt and mix well. Reduce the heat to low and cook for 1–2 minutes, until they are well combined and the millet is heated through. Remove from heat and serve hot. Refrigerated, this keeps well for 3 days.

Barley

Cooking Time
50 mins

Serves
4

Ingredients

3 cups Water
1 cup Barley, washed and soaked for 2 hours

Method

1. Over medium-high heat, bring the water to a boil in a saucepan. Reduce the heat and add the soaked barley. Cover the saucepan with a lid and cook for 35 minutes, or until the water has evaporated.
2. Remove from heat. Stir the barley, cover the saucepan and let it stand for another 8–10 minutes. Refrigerated, this keeps well for 3 days.

Variation

Mix 2 Tbsp kasundi mustard (Bengali mustard), along with a generous squeeze of lemon and chopped coriander leaves with the cooked hot barley. Kasundi is very pungent in taste and I recommend that you give it a taste before mixing the mustard into the barley.

Barley with Coconut, Cashews and Figs

Cooking Time
10 mins

Serves
4

Ingredients

- 2½ Tbsp Ghee
- 1½ Tbsp Coriander seeds
- ¼ cup Cashews
- ⅓ cup Thinly sliced fresh coconut,
- ¼ cup Dried figs, halved or quartered
- 2 cups Cooked barley (recipe on facing page)
- Salt, to taste

Method

1. Place the ghee in a pan, over medium-high heat. Once the ghee is hot, add the coriander seeds and let them splutter.
2. Add the cashews, stirring continuously for 3 minutes, or until they turn golden.
3. Add the sliced coconut and figs and cook for 3–4 minutes.
4. Add the cooked barley and mix well. Season with salt and remove from heat. Serve hot.

Tomato Barley

Cooking Time
20 mins

Serves
4

Ingredients

- 2 Tbsp Ghee
- 2 tsp Mustard seeds
- 4–6 Garlic cloves, finely chopped
- 4 Green chillies, slit lengthwise
- 2 sprigs Curry leaves
- 200 ml Tomato purée
- 2 cups Cooked barley (recipe on facing page)
- Salt, to taste

Method

1. Place the ghee in a pan, over medium-high heat. Once the ghee is hot, add the mustard seeds and let them splutter.
2. Add the chopped garlic, green chillies and curry leaves, and fry for 2 minutes, till the garlic is translucent.
3. Tip in the tomato purée and cook for 12–15 minutes, until the moisture dries up.
4. Add the cooked barley and salt. Mix well until the barley is combined with the tomato purée. Remove from heat. Serve hot. Refrigerated, this keeps well for 2 days.

Kheti Polenta

Vegetable polenta

Cooking Time

45-50 mins

Serves

4

Ingredients

4½ cups	Water
	Salt, to taste
1½ cups	Polenta
2 Tbsp	Olive oil or butter + 1 tsp olive oil
½ cup	Heavy cream
½ tsp	Turmeric
1 tsp	Red chilli powder
1 tsp	Coriander powder
1 tsp	Cumin powder
8–10	Snow peas
½ cup	Green peas
12–15	French beans
	Black pepper powder, to taste

Method

1. In a large pot over medium-high heat, bring 4½ cups water to a boil with salt. Add the polenta gradually, stirring continuously. This will prevent lumps forming in the polenta. On medium-high heat, continue stirring and scraping the bottom for 5 minutes, until the mixture thickens and starts spitting. Add the heavy cream and mix well. Reduce the heat to low, continue to cook for 1–2 minutes, stirring continuously. Remove from heat.
2. In a separate pan, heat the olive oil or butter on low heat. Add the tumeric, red chilli powder, coriander powder and cumin powder and fry for 1–2 minutes. Remove from heat and add the temper to the cooked polenta. Mix well to combine.
3. To blanch the vegetables, bring a pot of water to a boil over medium heat. Add a generous amount of salt to it. Meanwhile, fill a large bowl with ice water and set aside.
4. Drop in the vegetables, one at time. Let the vegetables cook in the water, till they turn bright green. The snow peas and green peas will take 2–3 minutes, and the French beans will be done in 3–4 minutes. Using a slotted spoon, remove the vegetables and add to ice water. Chill the vegetables for the same amount as they were boiled.
5. Drain the vegetables in a colander. Transfer them into a bowl and season lightly with salt and pepper. Add 1 tsp olive oil and mix. Top the creamy polenta with these crunchy vegetables. Serve warm.

Poha

Spiced flattened rice

Cooking Time

15 mins

Serves

4

Ingredients

¼ cup Cooking oil
1 tsp Cumin seeds
½ tsp Black mustard seeds
½ cup Peanuts
1 pinch Asafoetida
15–20 Curry leaves
1 Medium-sized onion, diced
2 Green chillies, chopped
200 gm Potatoes, cubed
1 tsp Dried raw mango powder (amchur)
1 tsp Coriander powder
½ tsp Turmeric
½ tsp Cumin powder
¼ tsp Black pepper powder
¼ tsp Himalayan black salt/½ tsp regular salt
½ cup Water
2 cups Medium or thick flattened rice
Juice from 1 lemon
2 Tbsp Chopped coriander leaves

Method

1. Heat the oil in a pan over medium heat. Once the oil is hot, add the cumin seeds and black mustard seeds and sauté for 1 minute. When the cumin starts to brown and the mustard seeds stop spluttering, add the peanuts, asafoetida and curry leaves. Stir-fry for 2 minutes, or until the peanuts are roasted. Remove the peanuts and curry leaves from the pan and set aside.
2. Add the onion, green chillies, potatoes to the pan and stir-fry for a minute. Add the coriander powder, turmeric, cumin powder, black pepper and salt. Mix well and fry for 1 minute.
3. Now add ½ cup water and cover the pan with a lid. Cook for 5–7 minutes, or until the potatoes are soft.
4. Meanwhile, using a colander, do a quick rinse of the flattened rice and drain it completely. Do not overdo the rinse, as flattened rice can turn mushy and soft. Add the flattened rice to the pan. Gently mix. Let it cook for 4–5 minutes, and remove from heat. Let the poha steam in residual heat for 10 minutes.
5. Remove the lid, add the lemon juice and coriander and gently mix. Remove from heat. Serve warm. Refrigerated, this keeps well for 3 days.

Upma

Savoury semolina

Cooking Time

15 mins

Serves

2

Ingredients

- 1 cup Semolina
- 2 Tbsp Ghee
- 1 Tbsp Split Bengal Gram (chana dal)
- 1 tsp Mustard seeds
- 1–2 Green chillies, finely chopped
- 8 Cashews, split in half
- 2 Tbsp Peanuts
- 8–10 Curry leaves
- ½ cup Finely chopped onions
- ¼ cup Finely chopped carrots (optional)
- ¼ cup Green peas (optional)
- ½ cup Finely chopped tomatoes (optional)
- 2 cups Water
- Salt, to taste
- 2 Tbsp Finely chopped coriander leaves (divided)

Method

1. Place a pan on medium heat. Once the pan is hot, add the semolina and dry roast it for 3–4 minutes, until toasty and fragrant. Take care to stir the semolina continuously, so that it doesn't turn brown. Remove from heat and transfer it to a plate or bowl.
2. Heat the same pan on medium-high heat and add ghee.
3. Once the ghee is hot, add the dal and roast for few seconds. Add the mustard seeds, green chillies, cashews and peanuts. Stir them well for 3–4 minutes on medium heat, till the cashews turns light brown.
4. Add the curry leaves, onions and cook for 3 minutes until the onions turn soft. Add the carrots and green peas, followed by the tomatoes. Stir well to mix and cook for 2 minutes.
5. Add 2 cups water and bring it to a boil.
6. Season with salt and 1 Tbsp coriander leaves. Gradually add the semolina in small batches and stir it continuously to avoid lumps. When the semolina absorbs all the water, cover and cook for 1–2 minutes. Remove from heat. Garnish with the rest of the coriander leaves and serve hot.

Sol Kadhi Khichdi

Kokum and coconut milk khichdi

Cooking Time

35 mins

Serves

4

Ingredients

15	Dried kokum pieces
1 cup	Water
1 Tbsp	Cooking oil
1 tsp	Mustard seeds
2 tsp	Chopped ginger
½ tsp	Cumin seeds
1 sprig	Curry leaves
2	Dried Kashmiri red chillies
1 pinch	Asafoetida
2 cups	Cooked rice (p. 50)
2 cups	Coconut milk
	Salt, to taste

Method

1. In a medium-sized bowl, soak the kokum in 1 cup warm water for 20 minutes.
2. In a wide, deep pot, heat the oil over medium-high heat. Once the oil is hot, add the mustard seeds and sauté for 10 seconds, until they splutter.
3. Turn the heat to low, and add the chopped ginger, cumin, curry leaves, red chillies and sauté for 30 seconds.
4. Add the asafoetida and rice and fry for 2 minutes on low heat. Pour in the kokum water along with the kokum, and stir and simmer over medium heat for 2–3 minutes.
5. Add the coconut milk and salt, and mix to combine. Cook for 5–7 minutes, until the rice reaches a creamy consistency. Remove from heat and serve hot. Refrigerated, this keeps well for 2 days.

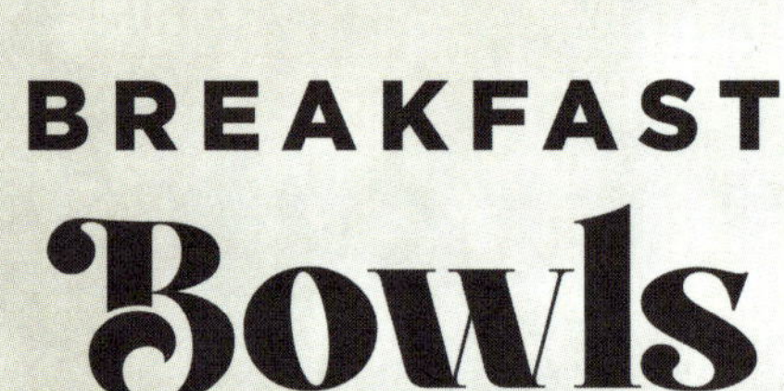
BREAKFAST
Bowls

Mango Yoghurt and Desi Granola

This delicious, creamy mango yoghurt bowl, topped with crispy Indian superfood grains can also be served as dessert, or eaten as an evening pick-me-up.

Cooking Time

25 mins

Serves

2

Ingredients

FOR THE MANGO YOGHURT

- 3 Medium-sized mangoes
- 2 cups Hung yoghurt (p. 11)/ Greek yoghurt
- 1 cup Mango pulp

FOR THE DESI GRANOLA MIX

- ⅓ cup Amaranth pops
- ⅓ cup Ragi flakes
- ⅓ cup Foxnuts
- ⅓ cup Pumpkin seeds
- ⅓ cup Quinoa pops
- ¼ cup Dried Coconut chunks

FOR THE GARNISH

- 3 Tbsp Mango chunks
- 2 Tbsp Black cherries (pitted)
- 2 Tbsp Chia seeds (soaked overnight in 4–5 Tbsp water)
- 1–2 Tbsp Honey

Method

1. Peel the mangoes and cut them into cubes. Add the cubes to a food processor and blitz to a smooth purée.
2. To make the mango yoghurt, mix the hung yoghurt with mango pulp and refrigerate overnight or for a minimum of 2 hours. The yoghurt keeps well for 2 days in the refrigerator.
3. For the desi granola mix, combine everything in a large bowl and set aside.

Bowl Assembly Arrange the mango yoghurt as the base of the bowl and sprinkle the desi granola mix on it. Garnish with fresh mango chunks, chia seeds and pitted black cherries. Drizzle the honey before serving.

Quick Tip Make a big batch of the granola and store in a an airtight container for a month. To ensure longevity, toast the coconut chunks before adding them to the granola mix. This ensures that the coconut does not turn rancid and spoil.

Saag Shakshouka

Shakshouka is a Middle Eastern breakfast favourite. I have made the dish my own by adding a mix of different greens that are in season and topping it with green chillies.

Cooking Time

30 mins

Serves

2

Ingredients

- 2 Tbsp Olive oil
- 1 Large onion, chopped
- 4 Garlic cloves, chopped
- ½ tsp Coriander seeds
- ½ tsp Smoked paprika powder
- ½ tsp Chilli flakes (optional)
- 400 gm Spinach (saag), chopped
- Salt, to taste
- ½ tsp Black pepper powder
- 2–3 Large green chillies sliced/8–10 Jalapeño slices
- 4–6 Eggs

Method

1. Heat the olive oil in a large pan on medium heat. Add the onion, garlic and cook for 6–8 minutes, stirring occasionally, until softened. Add the coriander seeds, paprika powder, and chilli flakes (if using), followed by the spinach and stir-fry for 3–4 minutes.
2. Add salt, pepper and a splash of water to the pan, cover and cook for about 10 minutes, tossing occasionally, until the spinach is very soft. If the spinach does not fit all at once in the pan, add in batches, until the spinach wilts.
3. Uncover and evenly spread the mixture across the bottom of the pan. Add the green chilli slices/jalapeño slices to the pan and mix well.
4. Use the back of the spoon to make four to six shallow indentations (depending on the number of eggs you are cooking) in the surface of the mixture to hold the eggs while they cook. Break the eggs into the indentations. Raise the heat to medium, cover the pan, and cook for about 4–5 minutes, until the whites are set but the yolks are slightly runny.
5. Remove the pan from heat. Drizzle a little more olive oil on top. Serve hot, directly from the pan.

Patna Poached Eggs

Poached eggs are my favourite way to eat eggs. I've given them a twist by serving them on a bed of Bihari aloo chokha with spicy garlic chutney. Feel free to substitute the aloo chokha with any leftover veggie preparation from your fridge – eggs taste good with everything.

Cooking Time

30 mins

Serves

4

Ingredients

FOR THE CHOKHA

- 2 Medium-sized potatoes, halved, boiled and peeled (p. 42)
- 1 Medium-sized onion, chopped
- 3 Green chillies, chopped
- 3 tsp Chopped coriander leaves
- 5 Garlic cloves, chopped
- Salt, to taste
- 1 tsp Mustard oil
- ½ tsp Lemon juice

FOR THE POACHED EGGS

- 4 Large eggs
- 2 Tbsp Vinegar
- Water, as required

Method

1. To make the chokha, mash the boiled potatoes in a mixing bowl. Add the chopped onion, chillies, coriander, garlic, salt and mix well to combine.
2. Heat the mustard oil in a pan over high heat. Once the oil starts smoking, take it off the heat and pour it on to the potato mixture. Add the lemon juice and mix well.
3. Crack one egg into a small bowl.
4. Bring a medium-sized pot of water to a gentle boil. Add the vinegar and stir the water so that it moves in a circular motion. Don't skip the vinegar, it is essential to help the egg coagulate in the simmering water. Without it, the white and the yolk will separate as the egg cooks.
5. Start by cooking one egg at a time. If you add more eggs to the pot, it'll be too crowded.
6. Gently, drop the egg into the water, give the water one more gentle stir, and cook 3½–4 minutes. Scoop the egg out with a slotted spoon and serve hot. Repeat this process for all remaining eggs.

Bowl Assembly Make a bed of the Aloo Chokha and place the eggs in the centre and top it up with Lehsun Mirchi Chutney (p. 19).

Quick tip Gentle is key when it comes to poaching eggs. Don't bring the water to an aggressive boil. Don't plop the egg in, and don't stir too hard. Working gently is the key to making perfect poached eggs.

Sabudana Khichdi

Tapioca pearls tossed with spices and vegetables

This delicious meal is especially popular in India during festive months when people are fasting. However, it is also a gluten-free, light and delicious meal – perfect to start one's day.

Cooking Time

15 mins

Serves

4

Ingredients

- 1 cup Tapioca pearls (sabudana)
- 1 Carrot, diced
- ½ cup Peanuts
- Salt, to taste
- 1 Tbsp Ghee
- 1 tsp Cumin seeds
- 10 Curry leaves
- 2 Green chillies, chopped
- 1 tsp Grated ginger
- 2 Medium-sized potatoes, boiled and cut into cubes (p. 42)
- 2 Tbsp Boiled green peas (p. 29)
- ½ tsp Lemon juice
- ½ Tbsp Chopped coriander leaves

Method

1. Rinse the sabudana well in water, until the starch is washed away. Transfer the drained sabudana in a bowl, and soak it in ¾ cup water. Cover the bowl and leave it for 3–4 hours or overnight. The duration for soaking these pearls will depend on their quality. I usually soak the pearls overnight.
2. The sabudana should be soft and easily mashed when pressed with one's fingers. If the center of the pearls retains some hardness, add 2–3 Tbsp water in the bowl. Cover and leave to soak for 30 minutes. Drain the soaked sabudana of all the water and set aside.
3. In a pan over medium heat, boil the carrots in 2 cups water for 3–4 minutes. Drain and put them in iced water for 2 minutes. Drain and keep aside.
4. In a pan over medium-high heat, dry roast the peanuts, until browned. Set aside to cool. Once cool, make a coarse powder in a mortar-pestle or in a dry grinder. Mix the coarsely powdered peanuts and salt with the drained sabudana.
5. Heat the ghee in a pan on low heat. Once the ghee is hot, add the cumin seeds and fry for 1 minute, until they crackle and turn brown.
6. Add the curry leaves and green chillies. Fry for 30 seconds and then add the grated ginger. Sauté for 30-40 seconds till the raw aroma of the ginger dissipates. Now add the potatoes, carrots and peas and sauté for a minute.
7. Add the sabudana. Cook on a low heat for about 3–5 minutes stirring often. When the sabudana pearls lose their opaqueness and become translucent they are done. Do not overcook the sabudana, else it may become dry and chewy. Remove from heat, add the lemon juice and chopped coriander leaves. Mix well.

Bowl assembly Serve the Sabudana Khichdi as is, or along with my favourite accompaniments, Pyaaz Aloo Bhajiya (p. 38) and Green Garlic chutney (p. 18).

Millet Falafel

Gluten-free, vegan and super healthy – these falafels offer up a great, nutritious start to the day.

Cooking Time

30 mins

Serves

2

Ingredients

- ½ cup Chickpeas
- 2 Spring onions, chopped
- 1 Medium-sized carrot, grated
- 5–7 Garlic cloves
- 9 sprigs Parsley or coriander leaves, chopped
- Salt, to taste
- 1 tsp Black pepper powder
- 1½ tsp Coriander powder
- ¼ tsp Turmeric
- 2 Green chillies (optional)
- ½ cup Cooked millet (p. 56)
- Cooking oil for frying

Method

1. To make the falafel, soak the chickpeas in cold water overnight, or for 8–10 hours.
2. Drain the chickpeas and add to a food processor. Add the spring onions, carrot, garlic, parsley, salt, black pepper, coriander powder, turmeric and green chillies in the food processor.
3. Blitz until the ingredients are evenly combined but still slightly course in texture. Transfer into a large mixing bowl.
4. Add the cooked millets to the chickpea mixture and season with salt. Oil your hands, and divide the mixture into 10 portions. Using the palms of your hands, shape the mixture into smooth balls.
5. Put enough oil into a frying pan or saucepan for deep frying over medium heat. Once the oil is hot, but not smoking – to check if the oil is hot, add a pinch of the mixture, if it sizzles immediately the oil is hot enough – add the falafels in batches.
6. Fry the falafels, without overcrowding the pan, for 2–3 minutes, or until they start to brown evenly. Remove with a slotted spoon and transfer to a paper-lined plate to drain.
7. For a healthier alternative, bake the falafel at 200 degrees C. Grease a baking tray with olive oil and line it with butter paper, add the falafels and bake for 8–10 minutes on each side.
8. To prep ahead, after step 4 place the shaped, uncooked falafels on a baking sheet-lined tray and freeze. Once they are frozen solid, add them to a Ziplock bag and store in the freezer. They last for 2 months, frozen. To use, leave the falafel out at room temperature for 2 hours, or until completely thawed. To cook, follow the recipe from step 5 onwards.

Bowl Assembly Arrange the Hummus (p. 23) as the base of the bowl and place the Millet Falafels atop it. To garnish go all out with any vegetables of your choice. I use avocados, cucumbers, onions, tomato chunks and gorgeous slices of candy cane beetroots. I also like to add a generous drizzle of chilli oil (optional).

Podi Idli Bowl

Steamed fermented rice cakes served with a lentil-spice mix

Idli is a favourite breakfast dish in India. Once the idli batter is ready, this is a quick cook. Make the podi ahead of time, stored in an airtight container it keeps well for up to 2 months.

Cooking Time

35 mins

Serves

4

Ingredients

FOR THE PODI

- 2 Tbsp Peanuts
- 4 Dried red chillies
- 1 Tbsp Split Bengal gram (chana dal)
- 1 Tbsp Skinned and split black lentils (urad dal)
- 1 1⁄ tsp Sesame seeds
- 1⁄ tsp Cumin seeds
- 2 sprigs Curry leaves
- 1⁄ tsp Jaggery
- 1⁄ tsp Salt

FOR THE IDLIS

- 1⁄ cup Skinned and split black lentils (urad dal)
- 1 cup Idli rice (parboiled rice)
- 1⁄ tsp Fenugreek seeds
- 1⁄ tsp Salt
- 2 tsp cooking oil, to grease the idli moulds
- 2 Tbsp Ghee

FOR THE SAMBHAR

- 3⁄ cup Split pigeon peas (toor dal)
- 6½ cups Water (divided), 6 cups at room temperature + ½ cup hot
- 2 Tbsp Tamarind
- 1 Tbsp Jaggery
- 2 Drumsticks
- 1 Tomato
- 10 Okra
- 1 tsp Cooking oil
- 12–15 Shallots (sambar onions), peeled and kept whole
- 2 cups Diced pumpkin
- 1⁄ tsp Red chilli powder
- 1⁄ tsp Turmeric
- Salt, to taste
- 2 Tbsp Sambar powder
- 1 tbsp Ghee
- 1⁄ tsp Black mustard seeds
- 1 pinch Fenugreek seeds
- 2 Dried red chillies
- 1 sprig Curry leaves
- 1 pinch Asafoetida

Method

1. To make the podi, heat a pan on medium heat. Once the pan is hot, add the peanuts along with red chillies and dry roast for 3 minutes, until the peanuts turn light brown.
2. Add the Bengal gram and black lentils and roast on a medium heat for 3 minutes. Add the sesame seeds, cumin seeds and curry leaves. Dry roast for 2 minutes, until the leaves turn crisp and sesame seeds smell toasty. Remove from heat and set it aside to cool.
3. Once the podi mix is cool, add them to a food processor along with the jaggery and salt, and blitz to a fine powder. Check the seasoning and add more salt if needed.
4. To make the idli batter, wash the black lentils and rice in separate bowls until the water runs clear. Soak them separately in plenty of water overnight, or for a minimum of 6 hours. Drain the water from both the bowls.

5. Rinse and soak the fenugreek seeds with ¼ cup water for about 30 minutes.
6. Drain the lentils and fenugreek seeds and add them along with 1 cup chilled water to a blender and blitz till the batter is thick, smooth, bubbly and frothy. To ensure that the idli batter does not turn hot or warm as that will result in dense idlis, use ice-cold water and grind in batches, if needed. This will allow the grinder to cool down between the grinding. Transfer the batter to a large bowl. You may need another 2–4 Tbsp water while blending.
7. Now add the rice to the blender with ½ cup water and grind to a slightly coarse batter. Pour this into the lentil batter. Mix both of them well with clean hands. Use your hand to mix as it helps to ferment faster and better. The batter must be thick yet of pouring consistency. Adjust and add more water, if the batter looks too thick.
8. Set the batter aside in a warm place for a minimum of 8 hours. Once the batter is ready, it will rise to double its quantity. In cooler weather, it may take up to 18 hours for the batter to ferment. To speed up the fermentation process, place the batter in the oven with the light bulb on, or preheat oven to 50 degrees C for 10–12 minutes and place the batter in the oven for 8 hours to ferment.
9. Alternatively, if you lack the time or energy to make the idli batter from scratch, store-bought idli batter is a great alternative. A 1 Kg idli batter pack will yield 17-20 regular-sized idlis. You will need 750–800 grams for this recipe. Refrigerated, the leftover batter will last for 3 days.
10. To make the idlis, bring water to a boil in an idli steamer. Grease the idli plates lightly with cooking oil. Mix the idli batter gently, not more than 1–2 times. Overmixing the batter, will turn the aerated batter flat. Fill the idli moulds with batter. I used a baby idli mould, but you can use a regular one and cut the idlis into pieces. The mix will yield 15 regular-sized idlis and 30 baby idlis.
11. When the water begins to bubble, turn the heat to low and place the idli mould in the steamer. Cover and steam for exactly 10 minutes on a high heat. Once the idlis are cooked, remove them gently with a spoon, place on a plate and allow them to cool.
12. Heat the ghee in a pan on medium-high heat. Once the ghee is hot, turn off the heat and add the idlis to the pan. Sprinkle 2 Tbsp podi on the idlis and gently turn the idlis over with a spoon to coat evenly with the podi.
13. To make the sambar, wash the lentils multiple times, until the water runs clear. Add the washed and drained lentils into a pressure cooker along with 2 cups water. Place the cooker on medium heat and pressure cook for 2–4 whistles. If using a pot, add 3 cups water and cook covered for 20 minutes. The lentils should be soft and mushy.

14. Set up a small bowl with the tamarind and jaggery. Add ½ cup hot water and let it steep for 15 minutes. When the water turns cool, mash the tamarind with your hands and remove the seeds and veins; discard. Set a mesh strainer over a clean bowl, and pour this liquid through it. Using a spoon, push out as much liquid and pulp as possible. Discard the remains from the strainer.
15. Scrape the drumsticks lightly with a knife and rinse with water. Chop them to 2-inch pieces. Dice tomatoes and chop okra to 1-inch pieces. Set aside.
16. Heat 1 tsp oil in a pot on medium heat. Once the oil is hot, add the onions and sauté for 1 minute. Add in the tomato, drumsticks, pumpkin, okra and sauté for 2 minutes. Stir in the chilli powder, and mix well. Pour in 4 cups of water and let it simmer on low heat for 10-15 minutes, until the vegetables are cooked.
17. Add the turmeric, salt and sambar powder. Add the tamarind-jaggery water. Cook this for 5 minutes on medium heat.
18. Mash the lentils with the back of a ladle, and add it to the vegetable pot. Let this simmer for 10 minutes, at this stage the sambhar will be at a gentle boil.
19. To make the temper, place a small pan with ghee on medium heat. Add the mustard seeds, fenugreek seeds and red chillies and sauté for 30–40 seconds, until the spices crackle.
20. Add the curry leaves and fry for 30 seconds, until the leaves turn crisp. Add the asafoetida, stir-fry for 20–30 seconds and pour this into the sambar. Remove from heat and serve hot. The sambar will keep well in the refrigerator for 3–4 days.

Bowl Assembly Arrange the idlis in a bowl and serve with Cucumber Thoran (p. 35) and Sambar.

Quick tip If sambhar onions are unavailable, you can use pearl onions or 1 medium-sized onion, quartered.

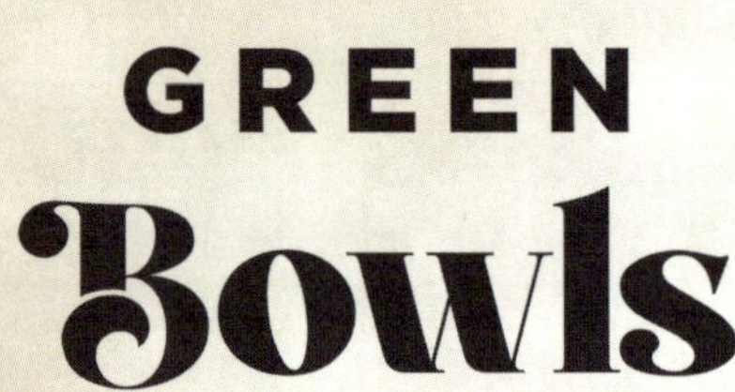
GREEN
Bowls

Achari Yam Tikka

Baked yam marinated in yoghurt flavoured with mango pickle

A healthier alternative to potatoes, these yam tikkas are a big hit whenever I'm entertaining at home. They work as starters, tossed into salads or when added to rolls and sandwiches. You can swap in sweet potatoes for a delicious variation.

Cooking Time

60 mins

Serves

4

Ingredients

- ½ tsp Turmeric
- 1 cup Cubed yam
- Cooking oil, for deep frying
- ⅓ cup Thick yoghurt
- 1 tsp Mango pickle
- ½ tsp Garlic paste
- ¼ tsp Deggi mirch, or red chilli powder
- ½ bunch Coriander leaves, chopped
- 1/4 tsp Kitchen king masala (optional)

Method

1. In a saucepan over medium heat, bring water to boil and add turmeric, followed by the yam pieces. Cook for 10–15 minutes, until the yam is soft and can be easily pierced through with a fork. Strain and set aside.
2. Preheat oven to 200 degrees C.
3. In a separate pan, heat the oil for deep frying. Add all the yam and deep fry on medium heat for 5–6 minutes, until they turn light golden. Place them on a plate to cool. If using sweet potatoes, skip this step and continue from step 4 onwards.
4. In a separate bowl, combine the yoghurt, mango pickle, garlic paste, deggi mirch and coriander leaves to form a marinade. Add the fried yam pieces and coat evenly.
5. Place the yam pieces on a baking tray and bake in the oven for 8–10 minutes, or grill until charred marks appear on the yam tikkas.
6. For a healthier alternative, you can skip step 3 and add the boiled yam to the marinade and bake for 12 minutes. If using sweet potatoes, bake them for 20 minutes.

Quick tip Take care to oil your hands and the knife before processing the raw yam. The peels of yam contain oxalate crystals that can cause itching – however, it can be avoided with this simple hack.

Bowl assembly Serve the Achari Yam Tikka with the Manipuri Black Rice (p. 51) and Beans Thoran (p. 35) and Coriander Salsa (p. 21). You can also serve the tikkas as is, with a chutney of your choice.

Rajma Galouti Kebab

Minced kidney bean kebab

A vegetarian take on the meat-based galouti kebab, this recipe combines the hearty flavours of kidney beans and delivers on the promised delicate texture of these famed kebabs. These kebabs also work well eaten as a wrap or as sandwich filling.

Cooking Time

45 mins

Serves

4

Ingredients

1 cup	Kidney beans (rajma), soaked overnight or for minimum 8 hours
4 cups	Water
	Salt, to taste
10	Mint leaves
2	Green chillies
1-inch	Piece ginger, peeled
8	Garlic cloves
12	Cashew nuts
2	Potatoes, boiled and mashed
1 tsp	Rose water
4	Saffron strands
1 tsp	Garam masala
1½ tsp	Chaat masala
1 tsp	Cumin powder
1 cup	Birista (p. 10)
2 Tbsp	Gram flour (besan)
	Cooking oil, as required
FOR SMOKING	
1 piece	Coal
1 tsp	Ghee
3	Cloves

Method

1. To cook the beans, drain them and add to a pressure cooker with 4 cups water and salt. Secure the pressure cooker lid and cook for 5–6 whistles. Turn the heat to low and simmer the beans for about 20 minutes.
2. Turn off the heat, and allow the steam to release from the cooker on its own. This will take 15 minutes. The beans should be tender and cooked through completely. Drain the excess water.
3. Grind the mint leaves, chillies, ginger, garlic and cashew nuts together in a food processor to a coarse mixture. Add the beans to the mixture and grind on the lowest setting till it forms a uniform mix. Scrape down the jar, if necessary.
4. Transfer this kebab mixture into a large mixing bowl. Add the mashed potatoes, rose water, saffron, garam masala, chaat masala, cumin powder, birista and gram flour. Mix well to combine. The mix should be firm and not crumbly, otherwise the kebabs wont hold their shape.
5. Place a hot coal in a small bowl, pour 1 tsp ghee and place 3 cloves on it. Cover the bowl tightly with foil or a lid, and place it inside the bowl with the kebab mix. Let the smoke infuse the mix for 5–7 minutes.
6. Divide the kebab mix into 8–10 equal portions. Apply oil to your palms, then shape the portions into 1-inch thick discs. Take care to patch up cracks, if any.
7. Heat a heavy-bottomed pan on medium heat and grease it with oil. Place the kebabs on the hot pan in batches. Drizzle a few drops of oil over the kebabs and pan fry them for 3 minutes on each side, until slightly crisp.
8. To freeze, after step 6 place the shaped, uncooked kebabs on a parchment paper-lined tray and freeze. Frozen, they last for 2 months. To use, leave the kebab out at room temperature for 2 hours, until completely thawed. To cook, follow the recipe from step 7 onwards.

Bowl assembly Serve with Millet Tabbouleh (p. 56), Raw Mango Salsa (p. 21) and Tomato Jaggery Chutney (p. 20).

Thecha-spiced Vegetable Stir-fry

Vegetable stir-fry with Maharashtrian peanut-chilli chuntey

A quick and delicious stir-fry recipe featuring thecha (peanut-chilli chutney) that can be made using any vegetables you have on hand.

Cooking Time

15 mins

Serves

4

Ingredients

FOR THE THECHA

- 1 tsp Cooking oil
- 6–7 Garlic cloves
- 3–4 Green chillies, roughly chopped
- 3 Tbsp Skinned, raw peanuts
- ½ cup Coriander leaves
- Salt, to taste

FOR THE STIR-FRY

- 1 Tbsp Cooking oil
- 8 Garlic cloves, finely chopped
- 1 Onion, sliced
- 1¼ cup Portobello mushrooms, sliced. (If using button mushrooms, cut them in half)
- 1 cup Red and yellow peppers, sliced
- 2 cups Chopped spinach
- Salt, to taste
- 1 tsp Black peppercorns, coarsely pounded
- 1 tsp Cumin powder

Method

1. To make the thecha, heat the oil in a pan on low heat. Add the garlic and green chillies and sauté for 30 seconds on low to medium-low heat. Add the peanuts and sauté for 2 minutes, stirring often until the peanuts become crunchy and crisp. Remove from heat and set aside.
2. In a mortar and pestle, add the peanut mix, coriander leaves, salt and crush to a coarse paste. Set aside.
3. To make the stir-fry, heat oil in a wok on medium heat. Once the oil is hot, add the chopped garlic and onions. Sauté for 2 minutes, until the onions turn translucent.
4. Add in the mushrooms and peppers and stir-fry for 3–4 minutes, on medium heat, until the mushroom starts to sweat.
5. Add the chopped spinach, salt, black pepper and cumin powder. Sauté for 3 minutes on medium heat, until the spinach is wilted and all the moisture has evaporated.
6. Add the thecha and mix well to combine. Cook for 1 minute. Check for seasoning and adjust if necessary. Remove from heat and serve hot.

Bowl assembly Serve with the Tomato Quinoa (p. 54) or Tomato Barley (p. 61).

Nani's Rajma Chawal

Kidney beans in a tomato-based gravy

The ultimate comfort meal for any North Indian. My nani, or maternal grandmother was from Jammu, a region that is known to grow the best rajma, and this is her signature recipe.

Cooking Time

60 mins

Serves

4

Ingredients

- 2 cups Kidney beans, soaked overnight and drained
- 8 cups Water
- Salt, to taste
- 2 Tbsp Mustard oil
- 1 Bay leaf
- 2 Black cardamoms
- 1 Two-inch innamon stick
- 3 tsp Ginger-garlic paste (p. 9)
- 4 Tbsp Brown onion paste (p. 9)
- 1½ cups Tomato purée
- 5 tsp Dried pomegranate powder (anardana powder)
- ½ tsp Turmeric
- 1 tsp Red chilli powder
- 1 tsp Cumin powder
- 1 tbsp Finely chopped coriander leaves

Method

1. To cook the rajma, drain and add to a pressure cooker with 8 cups water and salt. Secure the pressure cooker lid and cook for 5–6 whistles over medium heat. Turn the heat to low and simmer the beans for about 20 minutes. Remove from heat, and allow the steam to release from the cooker on its own. This will take 15 minutes. The beans should be tender and cooked through completely. Drain the beans and reserve the water for later.
2. Heat the mustard oil in a deep-bottomed pan on medium heat. Once the oil starts smoking, add the bay leaf, black cardamoms and cinnamon. Sauté for 30 seconds until fragrant.
3. Add the ginger-garlic paste and sauté on low heat for 30 seconds. Add the brown onion paste and sauté well for 2 minutes, or until the raw smell dissipates.
4. Pour in the tomato purée and sauté for 3–4 minutes, until the oil separates. Add the drained beans, the pomegranate powder, turmeric, red chilli powder and cumin powder. Sauté for 2–3 minutes.
5. Pour in the water in which the beans were cooked and simmer on medium heat for 6–8 minutes. Add salt, check seasoning and garnish with coriander. Remove from heat.
6. Refrigerated, the rajma will last for 3–4 days. You can make a big batch of the rajma and freeze it as well. Frozen, it will last for 2 months.

Bowl Assembly Place the Cumin Rice (p. 52) in the bowl and pour the Rajma on top and drizzle some hot ghee on it. Serve with Khatta Meetha Kaddu (p. 40) and Pomegranate Salad (p. 30). You can also serve the Rajma with Ghee and Chilli Millet (p. 57), Kurkuri Bhindi (p. 39) and Mint Yoghurt (p. 22).

Dal Tadka

Tempered lentil curry

This is a staple lunch at home during summers. Light, refreshing and easy to make.

Cooking Time

25 mins

Serves

4

Ingredients

- 1 cup Yellow pigeon pea (toor dal), washed and rinsed
- 4½ cups Water (divided)
- Salt, to taste
- ½ tsp Turmeric
- 2 Tbsp Ghee
- ½ tsp Black mustard seeds
- 1 tsp Cumin seeds
- ¼ tsp Asafoetida
- 3 Dried red chillies
- ½ tsp Kashmiri red chilli powder
- 1 Tbsp Chopped coriander leaves

Method

1. Add the rinsed toor dal with 4 cups water, salt and turmeric in a pressure cooker. Place over low heat and cook for 10 minutes.
2. Secure the lid of the pressure cooker and cook for 1 whistle on high heat.
3. Let the steam release from the cooker on its own. This will take 5–7 minutes. Open the lid and mash the cooked dal lightly with the back of a ladle.
4. Heat the ghee in a large pan over medium heat. Once the ghee is hot, add the mustard seeds, cumin seeds, asafoetida and dry red chillies. Let them crackle for 30 seconds.
5. Add the red chilli powder to the pan and immediately pour the cooked dal into the pan.
6. Add ½ cup water to thin down the dal and stir to mix. Check the seasoning and adjust, if required. Bring the dal to a boil and remove from heat. Serve hot.

Bowl Assembly Serve the Dal Tadka with Cumin Rice (p. 52), topped with Kurkuri Bhindi (p. 39) with a side of Kachumber (p. 30) and pickle. Or eat it with Rice (p. 50) and Jeera Aloo (p. 42).

Chana Dal Khichdi

One-pot rice cooked with split bengal gram and spices

This is my Dadi's recipe, and unlike the garden variety mushy khichdi, this produces a khichdi with a pulao-like texture. This can be eaten as is for breakfast, or served accompanied with yoghurt and pickle for lunch or dinner. But the real joy is in eating it with mutton curry, chutney and onions on a lazy Sunday!

Cooking Time

30 mins

Serves

4

Ingredients

- 5 Tbsp Ghee
- 1½ tsp Garlic paste
- 10 Black peppercorns
- 6 Cloves
- 3 Bay leaves
- 2 Black cardamoms
- 2 One-inch cinnamon sticks
- 2 Onions, chopped
- 3 Green chillies, chopped
- 1½ cups Split Bengal gram (chana dal)
- 1½ cups Rice, washed
- 1½ tsp Red chilli powder
- 2 tsp Cumin powder
- ½ tsp Turmeric
- Salt, To taste
- 3 cups Water

Method

1. Heat the ghee in a pressure cooker on medium heat. Once the ghee is hot, add in the garlic paste, and fry for 1–2 minutes, until the raw smell dissipates.
2. Add in the whole peppercorns, cloves, bay leaves, cardamoms, cinnamon sticks and sauté for 2 minutes, until fragrant.
3. Add the chopped onion, green chillies and sauté for 2–3 minutes, until the onion is translucent. Add the chana dal and fry for 3 minutes.
4. Now add the rice, red chilli powder, cumin powder, turmeric and salt. Mix well and pour in the water. Shut the pressure cooker and cook on high heat for 2 whistles. After the second whistle, lower the heat and let it cook until the third whistle. Turn off the heat. Let it rest for 5 minutes, then open the cooker. Serve hot.

Bowl assembly Serve the Chana Dal Khichdi with the Beetroot Yoghurt (p. 23), Mustard Baby Potatoes (p. 43), onions and papad. Or serve this khichdi with a meat preparation of your choice, such as Chicken Ghee Roast (p. 146) or Highway Mutton Curry (p. 174).

Paneer Tikka

Baked paneer in a traditional tikka marinade

This is a quick, delicious appetizer much loved across India. Boiling the paneer pieces in water for 2–3 minutes before marinating it will produce very, very soft paneer tikkas.

Cooking Time

25 mins

Serves

4

Ingredients

FOR THE MARINADE

- 1½ cup Hung curd (p. 11)/Greek yoghurt
- 1 Tbsp Ginger-garlic paste (p. 9)
- 1½ tsp Kashmiri red chilli powder
- 1 tsp Turmeric
- 1 tsp Cumin powder
- ¾ tsp Coriander powder
- ½ tsp Garam masala
- 1 tsp Chaat masala
- 1 tsp Carom seeds
- Salt, to taste
- Juice from 1 lemon
- 1 Tbsp Mustard oil
- 250 gm Paneer, cut into 1-inch cubes
- 1 Medium-sized onion, diced into 1-inch pieces
- 1 Medium-sized green capsicum, diced into 1-inch pieces
- Cooking oil, to brush on the tikkas

Method

1. Place the yoghurt in a large bowl, and whisk until smooth. Add the ginger-garlic paste, Kashmiri red chilli powder, turmeric, cumin powder, coriander powder, garam masala powder and chaat masala. Add the carom seeds, salt, lemon juice and mustard oil. Mix well to combine. Check the seasoning and adjust if required.
2. Add the cottage cheese, onions, capsicum to the marinade and gently mix until they are evenly coated with the marinade. Cover and refrigerate for a minimum of 2 hours.
3. Preheat oven to 240 degrees C.
4. Meanwhile, line a baking tray with aluminium foil or parchment paper, or grease it with oil. Arrange the paneer, capsicum and onions on the tray and brush some cooking oil on them.
5. Place the tray in the oven and grill for 5 minutes. Flip the tikkas and grill for another 5 minutes. Repeat for a total of 15 minutes, or until the edges of the paneer are charred.

Bowl assembly Serve the Paneer Tikkas with Kala Chana Chaat (p. 32). Garnish with chopped or spiralized vegetables of your choice. To make a wrap with these tikkas, add them to a tortilla or roti, add in lettuce, onions and a dollop of Green Garlic Chutney (p. 18) or Doon Chetin (p. 20).

Paneer 65

Batter-fried paneer sautéed with South Indian spices

Paneer 65 is the vegetarian version of the very popular entrée, chicken 65. Wondering where the 65 in the dish comes from? Some contend it was because the dish was invented in 1965 by restaurateur A. M. Buhari, while others claim it was item number 65 on a canteen menu for soldiers in Chennai.

Cooking Time

30 mins

Serves

4

Ingredients

- 3 tsp Ginger-garlic paste (divided) (p. 9)
- 1 tsp Red chilli powder
- Salt, to taste
- 25 Curry leaves, finely choped + 15 whole leaves
- 1 Tbsp All-purpose flour (maida)
- 1½ Tbsp Cornflour
- 1 Tbsp Rice flour
- Juice from 1 lemon
- 3½ Tbsp Water
- 300 gm Paneer, cut into cubes
- 3 Tbsp Cooking oil, for frying
- 2 Tbsp Red chilli sauce (such as sriracha)
- 1 Tbsp Tomato ketchup
- 1½ Tbsp Yoghurt
- 3 Green chillies, slit lengthwise

Method

1. Take 1 tsp ginger-garlic paste, red chilli powder, salt, curry leaves, all-purpose flour, cornflour and rice flour in a bowl and mix well. Add the lemon juice and 3½ Tbsp water and mix to make a thick, smooth, lump-free batter. Now add the paneer cubes into the batter and mix gently. Ensure that each cube is coated well.
2. Set up a plate lined with paper towels.
3. Heat 2 Tbsp oil in a wide saucepan on medium heat. Once the oil is hot, add and arrange the paneer pieces in a single layer. Once fried on one side, flip and cook the other side. This will take 3–4 minutes. Remove using a slotted spoon and drain on the paper towel-lined plate.
4. In a small bowl mix red chilli sauce, ketchup and yoghurt thoroughly. Set aside.
5. Heat 1 Tbsp oil in a pan on medium heat. Once hot, add 2 tsp ginger-garlic paste, 15 curry leaves and green chillies. Sauté for 2 minutes, until the raw smell of ginger-garlic paste dissipates.
6. Pour in the prepared sauce (step 4) and stir immediately. This will prevent the yoghurt from splitting. Let it simmer for a minute or so, and turn off the stove.
7. Allow the sauce to cool for 4–5 minutes, add in the fried paneer cubes to the sauce and mix well to coat the pieces evenly.

Bowl assembly My favourite accompaniments with Paneer 65 are Upma (p. 64), Koshimbir (p. 29) and Green Coconut Chutney (p. 16). But, Paneer 65 can be eaten on its own or with any grain of your choice, such as Rice (p. 50) or Peas Pulao (p. 53).

Paneer Kofta

Paneer balls cooked in a rich, creamy gravy

Paneer kofta is what vegetarian celebratory meals in North India are made of. These melt-in-mouth koftas can also be served as appetizers.

Cooking Time

45 mins

Serves

4

Ingredients

FOR THE KOFTA

- 1½ cup Grated paneer
- ¾ cup Mashed boiled potato
- 1½ Tbsp Gram flour (besan)
- ½ tsp Red chilli powder
- ½ tsp Turmeric
- ½ tsp Garam masala
- Salt, to taste
- ½ cup Cornflour
- Cooking oil, for frying

FOR THE CURRY

- 1 Tbsp Cooking oil
- 1 Bay leaf
- 1-inch Cinnamon stick
- 4 Green cardamoms
- 1 tsp Cumin seeds
- 1 onion, finely chopped
- 2 tsp Ginger-garlic paste (p. 9)
- ¼ tsp Turmeric
- 1 tsp Red chilli powder
- ½ tsp Coriander powder
- ½ tsp Cumin powder
- 2 cups Fresh tomato purée
- 2 Tbsp Yoghurt, whisked
- 1 cup Water
- 10–15 Cashews soaked in water for 15 minutes,
- Salt, to taste
- ¼ tsp Garam masala
- 1½ tsp Dried fenugreek leaves (kasuri methi)

Method

1. In a large bowl, combine the paneer, mashed potato, besan, red chilli powder, turmeric, garam masala and salt to form a uniform mix. Knead the mix well to form a smooth dough.
2. Divide the dough into 10–12 portions. Grease your palms with oil, and roll the dough portions between them to form small round balls, or koftas.
3. Place the cornflour on a plate and roll the koftas in it. Take care to coat them evenly.
4. Set up a plate lined with paper towels.
5. Heat the oil in a wok on medium heat. Once the oil is hot, carefully lower the koftas and deep fry in small batches. Fry on medium heat, for 5–7 minutes till the koftas turn crisp and golden. Place the koftas on a paper towel-lined plate, to absorb the excess oil. Set aside.
6. To make the curry, heat the oil in a deep-bottomed pan. Once the oil is hot, add the bay leaf, cinnamon, cardamoms, cumin seeds and sauté for a minute.
7. Add the onion and sauté well for 2–3 minutes, or until it becomes translucent. Add the ginger-garlic paste and sauté for another 2 minutes on medium heat.
8. Add the turmeric, red chilli powder, coriander powder, cumin powder and ½ Tbsp water so that they don't burn. Fry for 2 minutes. Add the fresh tomato purée and cover the pan with a lid. Cook for 10 minutes, until the purée thickens.
9. Meanwhile, place the cashews with 1 Tbsp water in a food processor and blend to a smooth paste.
10. Turn the heat to low, add 1 cup water, yoghurt, cashew paste and fry well. Now turn the heat up to medium and cook for 2 minutes. Season with salt and add the koftas. Cover and cook on low heat for 5 minutes. Finish with the garam masala and fenugreek leaves.

Bowl assembly Use the Ghee and Chilli Millet (p. 57) in the bowl as your base. Pour the kofta and gravy atop the millet and place the Saag (p. 45) on the side.

Jackfruit Biryani

Raw, unripe jackfruit is the star ingredient in this biryani. This unusual ingredient has a meaty texture that is often used as plant substitute for meat, and is much loved by both vegetarians and non-vegetarians alike.

Cooking Time

45 mins

Serves

4

Ingredients

- 500 gm Jackfruit, cut in chunks
- ½ tsp Turmeric
- 1 tsp Cumin powder
- 1 tsp Coriander powder
- ½ tsp Red chilli powder
- 2 Tbsp Cooking oil (divided)
- 1 Tbsp Gram flour (besan)
- Salt, to taste
- 4 cups Water
- 4 Green cardamoms
- 3 Cloves
- 2-inch Cinnamon stick
- 1 Bay leaf
- ½ tsp Cumin seeds
- 1 Black cardamom
- 2½ cups Basmati rice, washed and soaked for 30 minutes

FOR THE ASSEMBLY

- 2 Tbsp Saffron milk (Mix 2 Tbsp warm milk with 5–8 strands of saffron)
- 1 Tbsp Coarsely chopped coriander leaves
- 12 Mint leaves
- ½ cup Birista (p. 10)

Method

1. Place the jackfruit in a mixing bowl. Sprinkle in the turmeric, cumin, coriander, red chilli powder, 1 Tbsp oil, gram flour and salt. Toss the jackfruit to coat it evenly in the spices. Let it marinate for a minimum of 30 minutes.
2. To make the biryani rice, boil 4 cups water in a pan over medium heat and add the green cardamoms, cloves, cinnamon, bay leaf, cumin seeds and black cardamon. Add the rice. Take care to cook rice till it is 80 per cent done. This should take 7–8 minutes. Drain the rice in a strainer. Set aside.
3. Heat the remaining oil in a deep-bottomed pan on medium heat. Once the oil is hot, sauté the marinated jackfruit gently for 10 minutes, until it is cooked.
4. To assemble the biryani, in the same pan, spread the rice on the jackfruit. Top with the saffron milk, chopped coriander, mint leaves and birista. Cover and continue to cook for 4 minutes on a low heat. Remove from heat and serve hot.
5. Refrigerated, this biryani lasts for 3 days. Frozen, this lasts for 1 month. To reheat, thaw the biryani in the refrigerator overnight before reheating. Reheat it in a microwave or on the stove with a little water or ghee to retain moisture.

Bowl assembly I serve the Jackfruit Biryani along with Mirchi Ka Salan (p. 41) and Kala Chana Salad (p. 32). The biryani can be enjoyed on its own or with Burani Raita (p. 22) or Mint Yoghurt (p. 22).

Kadhi Pakora

Gram flour fritters cooked in a tangy yoghurt gravy

Though the Punjabis love their kadhi pakora and have made it their own, the dish owes its origins to Rajasthan. From there, kadhi travelled on to Gujarat and the Sindh region, on to its various unique regional versions across India. This is a Rajasthani recipe.

Cooking Time

60 mins

Serves

4

Ingredients

FOR THE PAKORAS

- 2½ cups Gram flour (besan)
- 1 cup Sliced onions
- 3 Green chillies, chopped
- Salt, to taste
- ¼ tsp Red chilli powder
- ¼ tsp Carom seeds
- ¼ tsp Baking soda
- Cooking oil, for frying

FOR THE KADHI

- 1 kg Curd
- 2 Tbsp Gram flour (besan)
- 1 tsp Red chilli powder
- Salt, To taste
- 2 Tbsp Ghee
- 2 Tbsp Sliced ginger
- 20 Garlic cloves, sliced
- 2 Onions, sliced
- 2 tsp Tumeric
- 1 Tbsp Coriander seeds
- 500 ml Water

FOR THE TADKA

- 1 Tbsp Ghee
- 10 Garlic cloves, roughly crushed
- 1½ tsp Cumin seeds
- ½ tsp Asafoetida
- 8 Dried red chillies

Method

1. To make the pakoras, combine the gram flour, sliced onions, green chillies, salt, red chilli powder, carom seeds, baking soda in a large mixing bowl, along with 3–4 Tbsp water. Mix well to combine – the batter should be sticky and thick.
2. For frying the pakoras, place the oil in a pan on medium heat. Test if the oil is ready, by dropping a small portion of batter into it. The batter should sizzle and come up to the surface. Drop small portions of the batter into the oil – as the pakoras will expand once dropped into the kadhi. Fry the pakoras in small batches, on medium heat. I like using my hands to shape and drop the pakoras into hot oil, but using a tablespoon works as well. Set the pakoras aside on a paper towel-lined plate to absorb the excess oil.
3. To make the kadhi, whisk the curd, gram flour, red chilli powder, salt and 1 Tbsp water together in a large mixing bowl.
4. Heat the ghee in a deep-bottomed pan and sauté the ginger and garlic for 2 minutes. Add in the onions and sauté till they are lightly browned. Add the turmeric and coriander seeds and sauté for 30 seconds.
5. Add the whisked curd mix and let this cook on medium heat for 3–4 minutes. Add 500 ml water and keep cooking on low heat till the kadhi thickens. Check seasoning and adjust if required.
6. Add the fritters to the kadhi just before serving and temper it. Heat the ghee in a pan on medium heat. Once the ghee is hot, add the garlic and let it lightly brown. Add the cumin seeds, asafoetida and whole red chillies. Sauté for 1–2 minutes, until the cumin crackles. Pour over the kadhi pakora. Serve hot.

Bowl assembly Like there are several variations of Kadhi Pakora, there are many personal favourite accompaniments. I love my Kadhi Pakora with Cumin Rice (p. 52), Lehsun Mirchi Chutney (p. 19) and Kachumber (p. 30). You can keep it simple and serve it with plain Rice (p. 50).

FISH AND SEAFOOD Bowls

Hing Prawn Pasta

The big flavour in this recipe comes from using asafoetida (hing) in the tomato sauce. The prawns can be swapped for any protein of your choice and for a vegetarian option, omit the prawns. Try this once, and you will be whipping it up on repeat.

Cooking Time

60 mins

Serves

4

Ingredients

- 4 Tbsp Olive oil (divided)
- 6–8 Garlic cloves, finely chopped
- ½ tsp Red chilli powder
- ¼ tsp Asafoetida
- 5–6 Tomatoes, puréed
- 6–8 Coriander roots and stems, finely chopped
- Salt, to taste
- ¼ tsp Black pepper powder
- 450 gm Spaghetti
- 400 gm Peeled and deveined prawns (I like jumbo prawns for this recipe)

Method

1. To make the sauce, in a heavy-bottomed pan heat 3 Tbsp olive oil on medium heat.
2. Turn the heat to low and add the garlic. Sauté till the garlic becomes translucent. Add the red chilli powder and asafoetida and sauté for 30 seconds. Add the tomato purée and coriander roots and cook for a minimum of 20–25 minutes on low to medium heat until the consistency thickens. Season with salt and black pepper.
3. Cook the spaghetti in a large pan of salted boiling water according to the packet instructions. When the pasta is ready, drain it in a colander, reserving a little of the cooking water.
4. Meanwhile, heat 1 Tbsp olive oil in a large frying pan on medium heat. Once the oil is hot, add the prawns and sauté for a minute. Add the prepared tomato sauce and simmer for 5-7 minutes on medium heat.
5. Add the spaghetti to the pan and toss it with the sauce, add a little of the reserved cooking water if the sauce needs to be thinner in consistency. Check for seasoning and remove from heat. Serve hot.
6. This sauce can be made ahead – refrigerated, this lasts for 4 days, and frozen it lasts up to a month.

Bowl assembly Place the Hing Prawn Pasta in a bowl and garnish with fresh basil leaves, if desired.

Quick Tip This sauce can also be served as a seafood stew. Add 400 gm prawns or fish in step 4 and cook until the seafood is done. Add the tomato sauce and cook for 5-7 minutes. Add 2 cups stock or water, and simmer to the desired consistency. For a vegetable stew, in step 4, sauté 1 cup broccoli florets, 50-60 gm butter beans and 1 cup chopped carrots until they caramelize. Add the tomato sauce and cook for 5-7 minutes on medium heat. Add 2 cups stock or water, and simmer to the desired consistency.

Megha's 15-minute Comfort Prawn Curry

This simple, delicious recipe using minimal ingredients is my go-to prawn curry when I'm feeling lazy. It is a mix of 2–3 regional Indian recipes and heavily inspired by the prawn malai curry that was on my restaurant, Lavash's menu.

Cooking Time

15 mins

Serves

4

Ingredients

- 1 Tbsp Cooking oil
- 2–3 Green chillies, chopped
- 2 tsp Chopped ginger
- 15–20 Medium-sized prawns, peeled and deveined
- 3 cups Coconut milk
- Salt, to taste
- 1 Tbsp Ghee
- 4 Red chillies, whole
- 1 tsp Mustard seeds
- 10 Curry leaves

Method

1. Heat the oil in a pan on medium heat. Once the oil is hot, add the green chillies and ginger and sauté for a minute.
2. Add the prawns and sauté for 1–2 minutes on medium heat.
3. Add the coconut milk, increase the heat to high and cook for a minute. Turn down the heat to medium, add salt and cook for 4–5 minutes.
4. In a separate pan, heat the ghee on high heat. Add in the red chillies, mustard seeds and curry leaves. Sauté for 1 minute, until the mustard starts to crackle and the curry leaves turn crisp. Pour this temper on top of the prawn curry. Serve hot.

Bowl assembly Serve the Prawn Curry with the Kasundi Barley (p. 60) and pair with the Rocket and Candy Cane Beetroot Salad (p. 33).

Rawa Fried Prawns

Semolina-coated fried prawns

This Mangalore-meets-Goa recipe results in the crispiest prawns ever. Serve this as a snack on rainy evenings or as a starter while entertaining at home. The recipe works just as well with any white fish.

Cooking Time

30 mins

Serves

4

Ingredients

- 4 Tbsp Ginger-garlic paste (p. 9)
- 2 tsp Turmeric
- 2 tsp Red chilli powder (divided)
- 2 tsp Coriander powder
- 2 tsp Cooking oil for the marinade + 4 Tbsp for frying
- Salt, to taste
- 10–15 Medium-sized prawns, cleaned and deveined
- 1 Egg
- 1 Tbsp Rice flour
- 50 gm Breadcrumbs
- 50 gm Semolina

Method

1. In a bowl, mix ginger-garlic paste, turmeric, 1 tsp red chilli powder, coriander powder, 2 tsp oil and season to taste with salt. Add the prawns into this marinade and refrigerate for 20 minutes.
2. In another bowl, crack an egg. Add the rice flour and ¼ tsp salt, and mix well to combine.
3. In a plate, mix breadcrumbs, semolina, 1 tsp red chilli powder and ¼ tsp salt.
4. Take the marinated prawns and dip each piece in the egg mix. Next, roll each piece in the breadcrumb mix. Refrigerate the prepped prawns for 10 minutes.
5. Place a pan on medium heat and add oil to deep fry the prawns. Once the oil gets hot, turn the heat down to low and add the prawns in batches and fry for 3–4 minutes, until they are golden brown.

Bowl assembly Put a generous helping of Sol Kadhi Khichdi (p. 65) in your bowl. Arrange the fried prawns on top of the khichdi and add Mango Kachumber (p. 30).

Lehsuni Prawn Tikka

This is my favourite tikka recipe. The fried garlic adds a bold punch and a depth of flavour to the fish. I also make the same recipe with chicken and use paneer for vegetarians.

Cooking Time

30 mins

Serves

2

Ingredients

- ½ cup Cooking oil
- 15 Garlic cloves, chopped into ¼-inch pieces
- ¼ cup Yoghurt
- ¼ tsp Red chilli powder
- ½ tsp Roasted cumin powder (p. 11)
- 1 tsp Carom seeds
- 1 tsp Ginger-garlic paste (p. 9)
- ½ tsp Green chillies, finely chopped
- 1 Tbsp Gram flour (besan)
- 1 Tbsp Lemon juice
- Salt, to taste
- ¼ tsp Black salt
- 1 Tbsp Mustard oil
- 200 gm Prawns, cleaned and deveined
- 2 Tbsp Melted butter

Method

1. To make the fried garlic, heat the oil in a pan on medium heat. When the oil is hot, add the chopped garlic and fry while stirring continuously on medium heat for 3–4 minutes or until the garlic is a pale golden colour.
2. Using a strainer, strain the garlic and oil. Spread the garlic pieces on paper towels and lightly sprinkle with salt. This can be stored in an airtight container for 2 months.
3. Place the fried garlic in a large bowl and add yoghurt, red chilli powder, cumin powder, carom seeds, ginger garlic paste, green chillies, gram flour, lemon juice, salt, black salt and mustard oil. Mix well.
4. Add the prawns to this bowl and coat it with the marinade. Cover the bowl and refrigerate for a minimum of 20–30 minutes, or preferably an hour.
5. Preheat oven to 180 degrees C.
6. Grease a baking tray with cooking oil and place the prawns on the tray and brush on the melted butter evenly. Bake this for 7–8 minutes, until the prawns are cooked.

Bowl assembly Serve the Lehsuni Prawn Tikka with the Beetroot Carpaccio (p. 32) and a helping of Upma (p. 64). Or pair it with Pomegranate Salad (p. 30) and Kheti Polenta (p. 62).

Kasundi and Coconut Prawns

Mustard and coconut prawns

A quick, no fuss, sautéed prawns recipe with the punch of Bengali mustard and the creaminess of coconut milk. This makes for a delicious wrap filling too.

Cooking Time

10-12 mins

Serves

4

Ingredients

- 200 gm Prawns (8–10 count size), cleaned and deveined
- 1 tsp Ginger paste
- ½ tsp Turmeric
- Salt, to taste
- 2 Tbsp Kasundi (Bengali mustard)
- ½ Tbsp Coconut oil
- 1 cup Thick coconut milk

Method

1. Wash and pat dry the prawns. Marinate with the ginger paste, turmeric, salt and kasundi for 5 minutes.
2. Heat the oil in a pan on medium heat. Once the oil is hot, add the marinated prawns and sauté for 2–3 minutes.
3. Add the coconut milk and cook on medium heat for another 3–4 minutes, until the prawns are cooked. The coconut milk will reduce to a sauce and coat the prawns.

Bowl Assembly Serve the Kasundi and Coconut Prawns with Sprouts Kachumber (p. 30) and halved Pickled Baby Onions (p. 28). This is optional, but I love to eat this with a fried papad.

Quick Tip To make a wrap, add the prawns in a roti or a tortilla. Add lettuce, or rocket leaves, thinly sliced Pickled Baby Onions (p. 28) and Lehsun Mirchi Chutney (p. 19) or Tomato Jaggery Chutney (p. 20).

Meen Moilee

Fish curry

A beloved fish curry from Kerala.

Cooking Time

30 mins

Serves

4

Ingredients

- 4 Tbsp Coconut oil
- 2-inch Ginger piece, very finely chopped
- 3 sprigs Curry leaves
- 2 Onions, finely chopped
- 6 Garlic cloves, finely chopped
- 3 Green chillies, chopped
- 2 Tomatoes, finely chopped
- 1½ tsp Salt
- 1 tsp Turmeric
- 1 tsp Red chilli powder
- 2 cups Water (divided)
- 500 gm Fish steaks (You can use any firm, flaky white fish. I use Surmai/King fish)
- 250 ml Coconut milk
- 1 tsp Vinegar

Method

1. Heat the coconut oil in a pan on medium heat. Once the oil is hot, add the ginger and curry leaves. Sauté for a minute.
2. Add the finely chopped onions, garlic and green chillies. Sauté for 2–3 minutes, until the onions are translucent.
3. Add in the finely chopped tomatoes and salt and fry until the oil separates. This will take about 5 minutes on a medium heat.
4. Add the turmeric and chilli powder. Sauté for 30 seconds. Add 1 cup water and let it come to a boil. Once the water boils, add the fish.
5. Let this simmer for 5 minutes on medium heat.
6. Reduce the heat to low. Add the coconut milk and the remaining water. Add the vinegar and simmer for 5 minutes. Remove from heat and serve hot.

Bowl assembly Place the Brown Rice (p. 50) as the base of your bowl. Top it up with the Beans Thoran (p. 35) and the Meen Moilee.

Chatterjee Family's Macher Paturi

Mustard fish wrapped and cooked in banana leaf

A signature Bengali preparation, this is a family recipe from my colleague, Shridula's home. She was generous enough to share it with me and now this is a favourite at my home too.

Cooking Time

45 mins

Serves

4

Ingredients

- 3 Tbsp Black mustard seeds
- 3 Tbsp Yellow mustard seeds
- 3 Green chillies
- 3½ Tbsp Mustard oil (divided)
- ¼ tsp Turmeric
- Salt, to taste
- 300 gm Barramundi (Bhetki) fish fillet, cut into 50 gm pieces
- 1 Banana leaf
- 2 Green chillies, slit lengthwise in half

Method

1. Combine the mustard seeds and soak in 1 cup room temperature water for 1 hour.
2. Place the soaked mustard, green chillies, 1 Tbsp mustard oil and turmeric in a food processor with 2 Tbsp water, adding the water a little at a time. Blitz to a smooth paste. You may need to scrap the mixture from the sides of the mixer jar at intervals. Season the mustard paste with salt.
3. Wash the Bhetki pieces and pat them dry. Coat the fish fillets with the marinade and let it rest for 15–20 minutes.
4. Wash and cut up the banana leaf into six 20 cm x 50 cm rectangular sheets. Gently toast them on a pan set on medium heat. This will ensure that the leaves don't crack when folded. Remove from heat and set aside.
5. Place the banana leaves on a plate and add one piece of fish on one leaf and top it with a slit green chilli and drizzle 1 tsp raw mustard oil on it. Carefully wrap the fish with the banana leaf in the shape of a well-sealed parcel. Use a cotton thread to secure the parcel/paturi or stick a toothpick where the two ends of the leaf meet when folded.
6. Place a frying pan on medium heat. Coat the pan with ½ Tbsp oil and place the paturis on the pan and cook for 10 minutes.
7. You can also steam the paturis. In a steamer, place the parcels in a single layer and steam for 10 minutes.

Bowl Assembly Serve the Macher Paturi with Rice (p. 50), Black Lentil Salad (p. 31) and Tomato and Jaggery Chutney (p. 20). If you would like to skip eating carbs with the paturi, serve it with Nimbu Mirch Broccoli (p. 44) and Aam Ki Launji (p. 17) on the side.

Pan-fried Pomfret

A juicy and succulent pomfret coated in a spicy lip-smacking marinade. It is healthy and super quick to put together too.

Cooking Time

30 mins

Serves

4

Ingredients

- 4 Small pomfrets (100–120 gm each)
- Zest from 1 lemon
- ½ Tbsp Honey
- 1 tsp Cumin powder
- 1 Tbsp Soy sauce
- 2 tsp Garlic paste
- 2 tsp Lemon juice
- ½ cup Chopped coriander leaves
- Salt, to taste
- 4 Tbsp Cooking oil (divided)

Method

1. Wash the pomfret and pat dry. There should be no moisture on the fish. Using a knife, make slits to allow the marinade to soak in well.
2. Add the lemon zest, honey, cumin powder, soy sauce, garlic paste, lemon juice, chopped coriander leaves and salt in a large bowl and mix well to combine. Add the pomfrets to this and marinate for 1 hour in the refrigerator.
3. To pan-fry one pomfret, heat 1 Tbsp oil in a pan on a medium heat. Add the fish, and shake the pan a little, to ensure that the marinade and fish do not stick to the pan. Add ½ Tbsp oil if you feel that the oil is not enough. You can also fry the fish in batches, ensure that they are not placed in a manner where they stick together, else they will get soggy.
4. Cook the fish for 4–5 minutes on each side. Serve hot.
5. Alternatively, you can slice the fish, marinate and pan-fry it. To cook only one serving, quarter the ingredients for the marinade.

Bowl Assembly Serve the Pan-fried Pomfret with Tomato Quinoa (p. 54) and Saag (p. 45). Or simply serve it with a salad of your choice.

Salmon Tikka

This is one of my favourite recipes. You can swap the salmon for any other lean fish or prawns.

Cooking Time

45 mins

Serves

2

Ingredients

- 2 Tbsp Mustard oil
- 3 tsp Red chilli powder (divided)
- 1 tsp Cumin powder
- 1½ tsp Garam masala
- 5 tsp Ginger-garlic paste (p. 9)
- 2 cups Hung yoghurt (p. 11)
- Juice from 2 lemons
- 1½ tsp Dried fenugreek leaves (Kasuri methi)
- Salt, to taste
- 1 Salmon fillet, cut into 50 gm pieces
- 2 tsp Salted butter, melted

Method

1. Heat the mustard oil on a pan on high heat. Once the mustard oil is hot, remove from heat and set aside.
2. In a big bowl, add 1½ tsp red chilli powder, cumin powder, garam masala, smoked mustard oil, ginger-garlic paste, hung yoghurt, lemon juice, fenugreek leaves, salt and mix well to combine.
3. Add the salmon pieces into the marinade and coat evenly. Set this aside in the refrigerator to marinate for a minimum of 2 hours.
4. Mix the butter and 1½ tsp red chilli powder together for basting and keep aside.
5. Preheat oven to 200 degrees C.
6. Take a baking tray, grease it with a little oil and arrange the marinated fish pieces on it. Bake for 15–20 minutes, till the salmon is cooked. Keep brushing the fish lightly with the butter mixture every 5 minutes.
7. To make this on a stovetop, place a skillet on medium heat. Once the skillet is hot, add the fish tikkas. Cover with a lid and cook the fish for 7–9 minutes. Remove the lid, flip the tikkas and baste with the butter. Cover again and cook for another 7–9 minutes.

Bowl Assembly Place the Poha (p. 63) as the base for the bowl. Serve with the Nimbu Mirchi Broccoli (p. 44) and Litchi Mirchi Chutney (p. 19). You can serve this on its own with any salad of your choice or roll it up in a tortilla or stuff it in pita bread with some lettuce, onions and any chutney of your choice.

Tamarind Glazed Fish

This grilled fish served with a delicious tamarind glaze makes for a quick, delicious weeknight dinner.

Cooking Time

20 mins

Serves

4

Ingredients

- ½ cup Tamarind paste
- ¼ cup Honey
- 1½ Tbsp Soy sauce
- 1 Tbsp Lemon juice
- 1 tsp Garlic paste
- 1 tsp Grated ginger
- ½ tsp Red chilli powder
- 1 Tbsp Coconut oil (or any cooking oil will do)
- Salt, to taste
- Black pepper powder, to taste
- 3 tsp Ginger-garlic paste (p. 9)
- 4 fillets River sole fish or any white fish, cut into 40 gm pieces (salmon or prawns also work just as well)

Method

1. To make the tamarind glaze, in a small saucepan, combine the tamarind paste, honey, soy sauce, lemon juice, garlic paste, ginger and chilli powder. Place the saucepan over medium heat. Stirring occasionally, cook the mixture for 5–7 minutes, until the mixture comes to a simmer and thickens into a glaze. Remove from heat and set aside.
2. In a mixing bowl, combine the oil, salt, black pepper and ginger-garlic paste. Gently place the fish pieces into this bowl and coat well. Let the marinated fish rest for 15 minutes.
3. Place a non-stick pan on high heat. Place the fish fillets in the pan. Cook for 4–5 minutes without moving the fish. Carefully flip the fillets and brush a generous amount of the tamarind glaze on the cooked side. Grill for another 3–4 minutes or until the fish is opaque and flakes easily with a fork.

Bowl assembly Serve the Tamarind Glazed Fish with Coconut Millet (p. 57), Purple Cabbage and Green Peas Salad (p. 29) and Aam Ki Launji (p. 17). Place the fish on the millet and drizzle some glaze on the fish before serving. This can also be eaten on its own, paired with a salad such as Rocket and Candy Cane Beetroot Salad (p. 33) or a side of vegetables, such as Sesame Snow Peas (p. 44).

EGG AND CHICKEN
Bowls

Dim'er Devil Bowl

Bengali-style spicy scotch eggs

Dim'er Devil is a cult classic from the Bengali snacking lexicon. The origins of this popular snack can be traced back to the colonial period when British influences blended with traditional Bengali flavours, to create unique dishes such as this one.

Cooking Time

30 mins

Serves

4

Ingredients

- 300 gm Chicken mince
- ¼ tsp Turmeric
- ½ tsp Red chilli powder
- ½ tsp Coriander powder
- ½ tsp Cumin powder
- 1 tsp Dried raw mango powder (amchur)
- 1 tsp Ginger-garlic paste (p. 9)
- 5 Eggs, hard boiled
- 2 Eggs, beaten (to coat and crumb)
- 2½ cups Breadcrumbs
- Cooking oil, for frying

Method

1. In a large bowl, add the chicken mince, turmeric, red chilli, coriander powder, cumin powder, dried raw mango powder and ginger-garlic paste. Mix well to combine.
2. Set up a plate lined with paper towels.
3. Divide the mince in 5 equal portions. Take a portion of the mince and flatten it across your palm. Place a boiled egg on the mince, and mould it around the egg – shaping it evenly from all sides. The prepped egg devil should be oval and egg-shaped.
4. Beat two eggs in a bowl. Coat each egg devil in the beaten eggs followed by a good toss in a bowl of breadcrumbs. Repeat dipping the devil in the egg wash, followed by the breadcrumbs. This will make the crust firm and sturdy. To ensure that the dry ingredients don't clump together, keep your 'dry' and 'wet' hands separate. Use your dominant hand to handle the breadcrumbs and non-dominant hand to dip the egg devils into the beaten eggs.
5. Heat the oil in a heavy-bottomed pan. To check if the oil is hot, drop a little piece of the keema into it. If it bubbles and rises up, the oil is ready.
6. Gently drop the devils (in batches) and deep fry for a minimum of 8–10 minutes, until they are evenly golden brown on all sides. Strain and place on a paper towel-lined plate to soak up the excess oil. Serve hot.

Bowl Assembly Serve the Dim'er Devil with a side of salad such as Mango and Rocket Salad (p. 34). Or serve this with my favourite accompaniments – Coconut Millet (p. 57) and Saag (p. 45). Serve with kasundi mustard (Bengali mustard) for that extra kick.

Midnight Chicken and Egg Fried Rice

This recipe is my go-to for those days when hunger strikes and time is scarce. Whether you're winding down after a long day or seeking a late-night indulgence, this bowl will do the job.

Cooking Time

15 mins

Serves

2

Ingredients

- 2 Eggs (divided)
- 1 Tbsp Water
- 1 Tbsp Salted butter
- 1 Tbsp Sesame oil
- 1 Onion, finely chopped
- 1½ cup Boneless chicken leg, chopped into bite-sized pieces
- 2 Tbsp Soy sauce
- 1 tsp Black pepper powder
- 2 cups Cold cooked white rice (p. 50)
- 1 tsp Cooking oil

Method

1. Beat 1 egg and water together in small bowl. Melt the butter in a large skillet or wok over medium-low heat. Once the butter is hot, add the beaten egg and cook for 1–2 minutes without stirring. Remove the egg from the skillet, shred into bite-size pieces and set aside.
2. Heat the sesame oil in the same skillet. Add the onion and stir fry for 3 minutes, until soft. Add the chicken, soy sauce and pepper and fry for about 5–8 minutes, until the chicken is cooked.
3. Add the rice and sauté. Cover and cook on medium heat for 3–5 minutes, until the rice is mixed well. Now add the shredded egg and take off the heat.
4. Top the rice with a sunny side up egg (optional). To do this, heat 1 tsp oil in a non-stick pan, and break an egg in a small bowl. Once the oil is hot, carefully pour the egg in the pan and cook on low heat for 2–3 minutes. Slide the egg off the pan carefully and place on top of the rice.

Bowl Assembly Place the Midnight Chicken and Egg Fried Rice in the bowl. Serve with Sesame Snow Peas (p. 44) and a fried egg. Garnish with fresh spring onion greens and add a dollop of crispy chilli oil, if desired.

Southern Style Egg Kurma

Cooked with coconut milk and a tempering of warm spices, this egg curry cooked South Indian Kurma style is an easy, comfort meal.

Cooking Time

45 mins

Serves

4

Ingredients

- 6–8 Eggs, hard boiled and halved lengthwise
- 3 tsp Coriander powder
- 1 tsp Turmeric
- 2 tsp Red chilli powder
- 1 tsp Fennel seeds (divided)
- 1 tsp Cumin seeds
- 2 tsp Grated ginger
- 6 Garlic cloves
- 4 Tbsp Water (divided)
- 1 Tbsp Cooking oil
- ½ tsp Fenugreek seeds
- 1 Two-inch cinnamon stick
- 2 Onions, chopped
- 2 Tomatoes, chopped
- Salt, to taste
- 600 ml Coconut milk
- Juice from 1 lemon

FOR TEMPERING

- 1 Tbsp Ghee
- 2 tsp Mustard seeds
- 10–12 Curry leaves
- 3 Dried red chillies
- 3 Green chillies, slit lengthwise

Method

1. Place the halved hard boiled eggs, yolk side up in a large dish.
2. Add the coriander powder, turmeric, red chilli powder, ½ tsp fennel seeds, cumin seeds, ginger and garlic in a food processor, along with 3 Tbsp water and blitz to make a spice paste.
3. Heat the oil in a pan over medium heat. Once the oil is hot, add the fenugreek seeds, the remaining fennel seeds and cinnamon stick and fry for a minute.
4. Add the onions and sauté for 3–4 minutes, until they turn light brown. Add the prepared spice paste and sauté for 3–4 minutes.
5. Add the tomatoes and salt and sauté for a minute. Add 1 Tbsp water and cover the pan. Cook the mixture for 15–20 minutes until the mixture looks thick and clotted, and the oil separates.
6. Now add the coconut milk and cook for 5 minutes. Finish with lemon juice – but add it in after turning off the heat or the gravy will turn bitter. Pour the gravy into the dish containing the eggs.
7. Prepare the tempering by heating the ghee in a tadka pan over high heat. Once the ghee is hot, add the mustard seeds, curry leaves and green chillies. Sauté for a minute and pour over the egg curry.

Bowl Assembly Pair the Egg Kurma with Barley with Coconut, Cashew and Figs (p. 61). Serve with a salad of your choice. You can also pair this with Brown Rice (p. 50), Carrot Thoran (p. 35) and Litchi Mirchi Chutney (p. 19).

Kohli's Butter Chicken

This recipe was the answer to my 2020 lockdown butter chicken cravings. This North Indian classic is among my most loved recipe reels on Instagram.

Cooking Time

45 mins

Serves

4

Ingredients

- 300 gm Hung yoghurt (p. 11)
- 2 tsp Garlic paste
- 1 tsp Ginger paste
- 2 tsp Red chilli powder (divided)
- 1 tsp Garam masala (divided)
- 1½ tsp Cumin powder
- ¼ tsp Coriander powder
- Salt, to taste
- Juice from 2 lemons
- 1 kg Chicken, curry cut or boneless
- 1 kg Tomatoes
- 2 Tbsp Cooking oil
- 200 gm Butter
- 2 tsp Dried fenugreek leaves (kasuri methi)
- Salt, to taste
- 2 Tbsp Heavy cream
- 1 tsp Vinegar, optional

Method

1. In a large bowl, add the hung yoghurt, garlic paste, ginger paste, 1 tsp red chilli powder, ½ tsp garam masala, cumin and coriander powder, salt and lemon juice. Mix well to combine and add the chicken pieces to this marinade. Let it marinate overnight, or for a minimum of 2 hours in the refrigerator.
2. To make the gravy, bring a pot of water to boil over medium heat. Drop the tomatoes in the water, and boil for 4 minutes. Using a slotted spoon, remove from the pot and let it cool. Place the tomatoes in a food processor and blitz to a purée. Set aside.
3. Heat the oil in a large pan over medium-high heat. Once the oil is hot, turn the heat to low and add the marinated chicken. Cover the pan with a lid and cook for 4–5 minutes.
4. While the chicken is cooking, start on the gravy. Place a frying pan on low heat and add the tomato purée and cook for 10–12 minutes, until it has reduced by ¼ parts and is thicker in consistency. The gravy should be thick enough to coat your spatula.
5. Add the butter, the remaining red chilli powder, fenugreek leaves, ½ tsp garam masala and salt. Cook for 5 minutes. Finish with cream, stir well and take off the heat.
6. Pour the tomato sauce into the chicken and cook for another 2–3 minutes. Taste the curry and add the vinegar if you feel that the dish could use some more sourness. Serve hot.
7. For a vegetarian version, swap the chicken with 500 gm cubed paneer.

Bowl Assembly Serve the Kohli's Butter Chicken with Cumin Rice (p. 52) and raw onion slices, cucumber or any other fresh salad of your choice. Or eat it with Kabuli Pulao (p. 53), Masala Onions (p. 28) and Kachumber (p. 30).

Chicken Thukpa

Himalayan chicken noodle soup

A perfect one-pot recipe for a cold chilly evening, every bite of this Himalayan dish is nourishing and delicious. The recipe might look daunting, but get started and it won't take longer than 30 minutes.

Cooking Time

30 mins

Serves

4

Ingredients

FOR THE CHICKEN BROTH

- 1 kg Chicken, curry cut
- 35 gm Ginger, sliced
- 10 Garlic cloves
- 1 Onion, cut into ½-inch dices
- ½ Tomato, chopped
- 2 tsp Salt
- ½ tsp Black pepper powder
- 2 Tbsp Soy sauce
- 3½ litres Water (divided), 2 litres room temperature water and 1½ litres hot

FOR THE SPICE PASTE

- 1 Onion
- 1 Tomato
- 6 Garlic cloves
- 3 Ginger slices

FOR THE NOODLES

- 250 gm Egg noodles
- 4 Tbsp Cooking oil (divided)
- 2 Carrots, julienned
- 1 cup Finely sliced cabbage
- 4 Pak choi/spinach leaves, whole
- 2 Spring onions, cut into matchstick-sized pieces

Method

1. In a large pot over medium-high heat, add the chicken, ginger, garlic, onion, tomato, salt, pepper and soy sauce along with 2 litres water. Bring the mixture to a boil, reduce the heat and let it simmer gently for 45 minutes to an hour to allow the flavours to develop fully. The stock can be made ahead and frozen for 4 months for future use.
2. To make the spice paste, place the onion, tomato, garlic and ginger in a blender and blitz to a smooth paste. This spice paste can be made ahead of time and stored in the refrigerator for 1–2 days, or frozen for up to a month for future use.
3. Cook the noodles according to the packet instructions. Once cooked, add 1 Tbsp oil to the noodles to prevent them from sticking together and set aside.
4. Once the broth has reduced, add 1½ litre boiling water to the pot and bring it back to a boil. Take off the heat and let it cool.
5. Strain the broth through a sieve into another pot, ensuring that the liquid is clear. Set aside. Remove the chicken from the broth and separate the meat from the bones, shred into smaller pieces and set aside.
6. Heat 3 Tbsp oil in a large pan on medium heat. Add the carrot and cabbage and sauté for 2–3 minutes until they soften slightly but still retain some crunch. You can add any vegetables you like, such as mushrooms, french beans, etc.
7. Add the spice paste and stir continuously, until the paste becomes fragrant, the mixture dries out a bit and starts to sizzle – this should take around 3–5 minutes.
8. Next, add the pak choi/spinach, chicken and spring onions. Cook them for 2 minutes. Pour in the chicken broth and allow everything to come to a simmer which will take about 3–5 minutes. Serve hot.

Bowl Assembly In a deep bowl, add a generous portion of noodles as the base. Ladle the thukpa broth over the noodles, ensuring that the vegetables are well distributed. Squeeze a quarter of a lime over the bowl, for a fresh, tangy kick.

Coconut and Raw Mango Chicken

I encountered this flavour combination during a culinary exploration of Kerala's spice trails, where home cooks proudly shared family secrets. A personal favourite, this recipe often makes an appearance when I crave something indulgent and comforting. For this recipe, I prefer using coconut milk powder over fresh coconut milk as it doesn't split.

Cooking Time

30 mins

Serves

4

Ingredients

- 500 gm Skinless, boneless chicken thighs, cut into 35–40 gm size pieces
- Juice from 2 lemons
- Salt, to taste
- Black pepper powder, to taste
- 1 Tbsp Garlic paste
- 2 Tbsp Ghee or coconut oil
- 1 tsp Black mustard seeds
- 1 tsp Cumin seeds
- 12–14 Curry leaves
- 2 Onions, diced
- ½ tsp Turmeric
- 1 tsp Red chilli powder
- 1½ tsp Dried raw mango powder (amchur)
- 400 ml Coconut milk
- 150 gm Raw, green mangoes, sliced lengthwise with the skin on

Method

1. Marinate the chicken in lemon juice, salt, pepper and garlic paste for a minimum of 4 hours.
2. Add the ghee to a non-stick pan and place over a medium heat. Once the ghee/coconut oil is hot, add the mustard seeds, cumin seeds and let them splutter for 30 seconds. Add the curry leaves and fry for 30 seconds.
3. Add the chicken thighs to the pan and allow to caramelize and brown all over. On high heat, cook the chicken for 2 minutes on each side.
4. Add the onions and turn the heat to medium. Sauté the onions for 2–3 minutes, until translucent. Add the turmeric, red chilli powder, mango powder, followed by the coconut milk. Cover and cook for 8–10 minutes on low-medium heat.
5. Now add the raw mangoes, season with salt and cover the pan with a lid. Simmer for 8–10 minutes, until the thighs are cooked through and the sauce has thickened. For a thinner curry, add hot water and simmer to the desired consistency.
6. This curry is best made with fresh raw mango. When in season, stock up on raw mangoes and freeze them to use whenever you are in the mood for this curry. Frozen, raw mango lasts up to 6 months.

Variation This curry can also be made using seafood. Use 500 gm prawns or any firm, white fish, add them after step 4 and cook for less than 5-7 minutes.

Bowl Assembly Serve the Coconut and Raw Mango Chicken with Tamarind Millet (p. 60) and Koshimbir (p. 29). Or pair this with Manipuri Black Rice (p. 51) and Cucumber Thoran (p. 35).

Tandoori Chicken

With a smokey flavour, vibrant colour and a spicy marinade – this crowd pleaser needs no introduction. Though tandoori chicken is often cooked in a clay oven or on an open fire grill, this recipe will yield great results even when using a grill, oven or a stovetop.

Cooking Time

45 mins

Serves

4

Ingredients

2 Tbsp	Mustard oil
1 kg	Chicken, curry cut
2 tsp	Red chilli powder (divided)
1 tsp	Cumin powder
½ tsp	Garam masala
5 tsp	Ginger-garlic paste (p. 9)
2 cups	Hung yoghurt (p. 11)
	Juice from 2 lemons
½ tsp	Dried fenugreek leaves (kasuri methi)
	Salt, to taste
1 Tbsp	Tomato paste (optional)
2 tsp	Salted butter, melted

Method

1. Place the mustard oil in a pan over high heat. Once the oil starts smoking, take off the heat and set aside.
2. Using a sharp knife, make deep diagonal cuts on the chicken pieces. This allows the flavours of the marinade to seep through the meat.
3. In a large bowl, combine 1½ tsp red chilli powder, cumin powder, garam masala, smoked oil , ginger-garlic paste, hung yoghurt, lemon juice, dried fenugreek leaves, salt and mix well. To make a dairy-free version, skip the curd and use 1 Tbsp tomato paste instead. Check seasoning and add the chicken in this marinade. Mix well to coat each piece evenly. Refrigerate for a minimum of 2 hours, or longer if time permits.
4. Preheat oven to 250 degrees C.
5. Combine the melted butter with the rest of the red chilli powder and keep aside for basting.
6. Grease a baking tray with a little oil and arrange the chicken pieces on it. Bake for 30–35 minutes, brushing the chicken lightly with the chilli butter. Baste every 5–7 minutes, until the chicken is cooked. For a dairy-free version, skip basting the chicken with chilli butter.
7. To make this on a stovetop, heat a heavy-bottomed pan with 3 Tbsp oil on medium heat. Once the oil is hot, add the chicken pieces and cover. Cook the chicken while regularly basting with the chilli butter. This will take 30 minutes.

Bowl Assembly Serve the Tandoori Chicken with Kheti Polenta (p. 62). Garnish with Sautéed Cowpea beans and Snow Peas (p. 44), Pickled Baby Onions (p. 28), chilli/paprika butter and garlic flakes – or serve these on the side for guests to pick and choose in case you are serving while entertaining. If you have leftovers, shred the chicken and add it to a salad or use it as a sandwich or wrap stuffing.

Quick Tip To intensify the smokey flavour, smoke the marinated chicken before cooking it. Take a hot coal in a small steel bowl and place it in the centre of your marinated chicken bowl. Add 2 cloves on the hot coal and pour 1 spoon ghee on it. Quickly cover and seal the bowl with foil for 10 minutes, to trap the smoke and allow it to seep into the marinade.

Chatterjee Chicken Cutlet

My 'mini' me at work, and the head chef at my restaurant Mezze Mambo, Shridula Chatterjee is family. She helped me put this book together and introduced me to this dish over dinner at her home. This is her recipe that I absolutely love!

Cooking Time

45 mins

Serves

4

Ingredients

- 500 gm Chicken mince
- 2 Green chillies
- ½ tsp Thyme leaves
- 1 tsp Finely chopped leeks
- 1 tsp Finely chopped celery
- 2 tsp Red chilli powder
- 1 tsp Coriander powder
- 1 tsp Kitchen King masala (optional)
- Salt, to taste
- 2 tsp Chopped garlic
- 2 gm Hot paprika powder
- 2 gm Sweet paprika powder
- 2 Eggs (divided)
- 2 cups Breadcrumbs
- Cooking oil, for frying

Method

1. Add the chicken mince, green chillies, thyme, leeks, celery, red chilli powder, coriander powder, Kitchen King masala (if using), salt, garlic, paprika powders and one egg in a large bowl and mix well to combine.
2. Lightly oil your palms and divide and shape the meat mixture into 10–12 lime-sized portions. Place each portion in the palm of your hand, and flatten them into ⅓-inch thick patties.
3. In another bowl, crack and beat the remaining egg and set aside.
4. Place the breadcrumbs on a plate. Using your dominant hand, dunk each shaped cutlet in the egg batter, and then using the other hand roll the cutlet in the breadcrumbs. Repeat this process to get a firm crumb and coating.
5. Heat the oil in a pan over medium heat and deep fry the cutlets for around 4–5 minutes, until golden brown.
6. Remove using a slotted spoon and place on a paper towel-lined plate to soak up the excess oil. To check if the cutlet is cooked, insert the tip of a knife in the centre of the cutlet for 5–10 seconds and if the tip comes out hot, it means the cutlet is cooked.

Bowl Assembly Plate the Chicken Cutlets with Jhatpat Aloo (p. 43) and White Kidney Bean, Mango and Rocket Salad (p. 34). Serve with kasundi mustard (Bengali mustard) or Pudina Dhania Chutney (p. 18).

Chicken Ghee Roast

In 2019, I went on a one-of-a-kind road trip across Karnataka with my mentor Chef Saby – we ate every two hours on that week-long trip. Among the many culinary memories from that trip, the flavours of this dish – the spice of the Byadgi chillies and freshly sourced cow ghee – have a permanent spot in my heart.

Cooking Time

45 mins

Serves

4

Ingredients

- 500 gm Boneless chicken leg, cut into 30–35 gm pieces,
- ½ cup Yoghurt
- Salt, to taste
- ¼ tsp Turmeric
- 1½ Tbsp Coriander seeds
- ¼ tsp Fenugreek seeds
- 1 tsp Cumin seeds
- ¼ tsp Whole black peppercorns
- ½ tsp Fennel seeds
- 2 Cloves
- 1 Two-inch cinnamon stick
- 12–15 Dried Byadgi red chillies (Kashmiri chillies can be used as a substitute)
- 12 Garlic cloves
- 15 gm Tamarind paste
- ¼ cup Water
- 2 Tbsp Ghee (divided)
- 4 sprigs Curry leaves (divided)
- ½ tsp Jaggery
- Lemon juice, as needed

Method

1. In a large mixing bowl, combine the chicken pieces, yoghurt, salt and turmeric. Marinate for at least 2 hours.
2. Heat a pan over medium heat. Dry roast the coriander seeds, fenugreek seeds, cumin seeds, black peppercorns, fennel seeds, cloves, cinnamon and chillies for 2 minutes, until toasty and fragrant. Remove from heat and set aside to cool.
3. Once cool, transfer all the roasted spices to a food processor. Add the garlic cloves, tamarind paste, ¼ cup water to the food processor and blitz to a fine paste. Set aside.
4. Heat 1 Tbsp ghee in a heavy-bottomed pan over medium-high heat. Once the ghee is hot, add the marinated chicken and cook for 4 minutes on each side. Remove the chicken from the pan and set aside.
5. To the same pan add 1 Tbsp ghee on medium heat. Once the ghee is hot, turn down the heat to low, and add 2 sprigs curry leaves and the ground dry masala. Stir and cook the masala for 12 minutes on low heat. Once the ghee starts to separate from the masala, add the chicken and mix well to coat each piece.
6. Cover the pan with a lid and cook for 5 minutes on low heat, or until the chicken is done. Take care to keep stirring in intervals to prevent the masala from sticking to the bottom of the pan.
7. Finish with jaggery, lemon juice and the rest of the curry leaves. Cook for 1 minute and remove from heat. Serve hot.

Bowl Assembly Serve the Chicken Ghee Roast with Idlis (p. 78) and Beans Thoran (p. 35). It also pairs well with Rice (p. 50) or Saffron Pilaf (p. 52). Or simply serve it as is, with a fresh salad of your choice.

Chicken Tikka

True crowd pleasers, chicken tikkas can be quite versatile. Serve them as appetizers, or stuff them in a wrap, or add them to a platter, you cannot go wrong with this recipe.

Cooking Time

45 mins

Serves

4

Ingredients

- 2 Tbsp Mustard oil
- 2 tsp Kashmiri red chilli powder (divided)
- ½ tsp Turmeric
- 1 tsp Coriander powder
- ¾ tsp Cumin powder
- ½ tsp Garam Masala
- 5 tsp Ginger-garlic paste (p. 9)
- 1 cup Hung yoghurt (p. 11)
- Juice from 1 lemon
- ½ tsp Dried fenugreek leaves (kasuri methi)
- Salt, to taste
- 500 gm Boneless chicken leg, cut into 40 gm pieces
- 2 tsp Room temperature salted butter
- 1 tsp Cooking oil
- 1 tsp Chaat masala

Method

1. Place the mustard oil in a pan over high heat. Once the oil starts smoking, remove from heat and set aside.
2. In a large bowl, combine 1½ tsp red chilli powder, turmeric, coriander powder, cumin powder, garam masala, smoked oil and ginger-garlic paste. Add the hung yoghurt and mix thoroughly.
3. Add the lemon juice, dried fenugreek leaves and salt. Check seasoning and place the chicken in this marinade and mix well to coat each piece evenly. Refrigerate this for a minimum of 2 hours, or longer if you have the time.
4. Preheat oven to 250 degrees C.
5. Mix room-temperature butter and the rest of the red chilli powder and keep aside for basting. You can skip adding the red chilli powder and use only salted butter to baste the chicken.
6. Grease a baking tray with 1 tsp oil and arrange the chicken on it.
7. Place the tray in the oven and cook for 15 minutes until slightly charred around the edges and cooked through. Brush the chicken lightly with butter after every 5 minutes until the chicken is cooked. Once the chicken is done, place in a large bowl, add the chaat masala and mix well.
8. To make this on a stovetop, heat a skillet on medium heat. Once the skillet is hot, add the chicken. Cover with a lid and cook the chicken, while regularly basting with the prepped butter. This process will take 15 minutes.

Bowl Assembly Serve the Chicken tikka with Lentil Salad (p. 31), Mint Yoghurt (p. 22) and raw sliced onions.

Yoghurt and Green Chilli Chicken Breast

A healthy, delicious and fuss-free meal option for all the protein lovers. I like to use skinless chicken breasts for this recipe but you can also use thigh or chicken drumsticks.

Cooking Time

25 mins

Serves

4

Ingredients

- 4 Chicken breasts
- 2 Green chillies
- 1 Tbsp Water
- ½ cup Hung yoghurt (p. 11)/ Greek yoghurt
- 2 tsp Garlic paste
- 1 Tbsp Lemon juice
- ½ tsp Red chilli powder/ 2 tsp Paprika
- Salt, to taste
- ½ tsp Black pepper powder

Method

1. Pat the chicken with a paper towel to ensure that there is no moisture on it.
2. Using a mortar and pestle, pound the green chillies with 1 Tbsp water to make a coarse chilli paste.
3. Place the yoghurt, garlic paste, green chilli paste, lemon juice, red chilli powder/paprika, salt and black pepper powder in a large bowl and mix well to create a marinade.
4. Add the chicken to the marinade and mix well to evenly coat. Marinate for a minimum of 30 minutes or up to 24 hours in the refrigerator.
5. Heat a griddle pan or a skillet on medium-high heat. Once the pan is hot, place the chicken and cook uncovered for 6–8 minutes on one side. Use tongs to flip the chicken and cook for 6–8 more minutes on the other side.
6. Transfer the chicken to a plate or cutting board, and let it rest for 2–3 minutes before slicing and serving.

Bowl Assembly Pair the Yoghurt and Green Chilli Chicken Breast with Rice (p. 50), Scarlet Kidney Beans and Tomato Salad (p. 33) and Mango Chutney (p. 17). Or serve this on its own, with Mango and Rocket Salad (p. 34) or any other salad of your choice.

Black Pepper Chicken Tikka

This delicious yet subtle, non-spicy kebab celebrates the king of spices – black pepper. The chicken can be prepped a day ahead, there is nothing more to this than placing everything in the oven and waiting for the results – and for the amount of work involved, the rewards are remarkable.

Cooking Time

45 mins

Serves

4

Ingredients

8	Garlic cloves
1	Green chilli
3 tsp	Whole black peppercorns
1 cup	Hung yoghurt (p. 11)
1½ tsp	Cornflour
½ tsp	Green cardamom powder
¼ tsp	Garam masala
	Salt, to taste
500 gm	Boneless chicken leg, cut into 35–40 gm pieces
1 Tbsp	Melted butter, for basting

Method

1. Blend the garlic, chilli and 1 Tbsp water in a food processor to a fine paste.
2. Grind the black peppercorns coarsely in a mortar and pestle. Set aside.
3. Place the yoghurt in a mixing bowl along with cornflour. Whisk well making sure there are no lumps. Add the garlic and chilli paste, ground peppercorns, cardamom powder, garam masala, salt and mix well to combine. Add the chicken to this marinade and mix well.
4. To marinate, refrigerate overnight, or for a minimum of 4 hours.
5. Preheat oven to 200 degrees C.
6. Brush a baking tray with a little melted butter. Place the chicken on the tray and cook for 15–20 minutes until slightly charred around the edges and cooked through. Turn the pieces half way through the cooking process and baste with butter.

Bowl Assembly Serve the Black Pepper Chicken Tikka with Tomato Barley (p. 61) and a salad of your choice. You can also serve these tikkas as is along with a dip. I like Green Garlic Chutney (p. 18) or Mint Yoghurt (p. 22).

Tangra Chilli Chicken

Originating from the Chinese community settled in Tangra, Kolkata, this Indo-Chinese dish is a beloved classic. Served as snack, starter or side, it blends Indian spices with Chinese cooking techniques, resulting in a perfectly balanced sweet, spicy and tangy chicken.

Cooking Time

30 mins

Serves

4

Ingredients

FOR THE CHICKEN

- 600 gm Boneless, skinless chicken thighs
- ¾ Tbsp Ginger paste
- ¾ Tbsp Garlic paste
- 1 tsp Kashmiri red chilli powder
- 1 tsp Salt
- 1 Egg, beaten
- ½ cup Cornflour
- ½ cup All-purpose flour (maida)
- ½ cup Water
- Cooking oil, for frying

FOR THE SAUCE

- 1 tsp Cornflour
- 1 Tbsp Cooking oil
- 8 Garlic cloves, sliced
- 2 Tbsp Soy sauce
- 2 Tbsp Red chilli sauce (such as Sriracha)
- 1 Tbsp Vinegar
- ½ cup Water
- 10 Green chillies, sliced lengthwise

Method

1. Cut the chicken in about 1-inch pieces. Wash and dry thoroughly.
2. In a large bowl, mix the ginger paste, garlic paste, red chilli powder, salt and the beaten egg. Add the chicken pieces to this marinade. Set aside for 2 hours.
3. Mix the cornflour and flour in a large bowl and add it to the chicken, creating a uniform coating. Add ½ cup water and ensure the chicken is evenly coated on all sides. Add more water if required.
4. Set up a plate lined with paper towels.
5. To deep fry the chicken, heat the oil in a wide-bottomed pan on medium-high heat. Once the oil is hot, turn the heat down to low and add the chicken in batches. Fry for approximately 6–8 minutes, turning them around frequently to ensure that they cook evenly, until they are golden brown. Remove with a slotted spoon and place on the paper towel-lined plate.
6. To make the sauce, combine the cornflour with 2 tsp water and prepare a slurry. Set aside.
7. Heat 1 Tbsp of oil over medium heat. Once the oil is hot, add the sliced garlic and fry for about a minute until pale golden. Add in the soy sauce, chilli sauce, vinegar, water, the cornstarch slurry and bring to simmer till the sauce thickens.
8. Add in the chicken, the sliced chillies and toss for about 2 minutes. Remove from heat and serve hot.

Bowl Assembly Serve the Tangra Chilli Chicken with Mango and Rocket Salad (p. 34). Eat with freshly fried Luchis (p. 45). The Tangra Chilli Chicken can also be enjoyed on its own, or paired with Manipuri Black Rice (p. 51) and Sesame Snow Peas (p. 44).

Chicken Korma

Braised chicken cooked in a rich, creamy sauce

In 2010, I met Irfan bhai, a tourist guide tasked with showing me monuments in Agra, but he ended up introducing me to the city's best hole-in-the-wall eateries. Since then, I have visited his home several times and I am obsessed with this korma he served me. He has graciously shared the recipe for this rich, creamy curry.

Cooking Time

45 mins

Serves

4

Ingredients

- 500 gm Chicken, curry cut
- 2 tsp Ginger-garlic paste (divided) (p. 9)
- Birista of 2 large onions (p. 10)
- 100 gm Cashews, soaked in water for 15 minutes
- 3 cups Water (divided)
- ½ cup Ghee
- 1 Two-inch cinnamon stick
- 1 Bay leaf
- 3 Green cardamoms
- ¼ tsp Cumin seeds
- ¼ tsp Turmeric
- ¼ tsp Red chilli powder
- ½ tsp Kitchen King masala
- ½ tsp Coriander powder
- 2 cups Water (divided)
- 4–5 Saffron strands, soaked in 2 tsp water
- 2 Tbsp Yoghurt
- ½ cup Fresh cream
- Salt, to taste
- ¼ tsp Green cardamom powder

Method

1. Place the chicken in a large bowl, and add 1 tsp of the ginger-garlic paste. Mix well to combine. Marinate the chicken for a minimum of 2 hours.
2. Reserve a little birista for garnish and add the rest of it along with the soaked cashews and ½ cup water in a food processor and blitz to a smooth paste.
3. Heat the ghee in a pan over medium-high heat. Once the ghee is hot, add the cinnamon, bay leaf, cardamoms, cumin seeds and sauté for a minute on medium heat. Add 1 tsp ginger-garlic paste and sauté for a minute on medium heat.
4. Add the onion-cashew paste and sauté for 2–4 minutes. Add the turmeric, red chilli powder, Kitchen King masala, coriander powder and fry for 30 seconds. Add ½ cup water and mix well. Fry for 1 minute, until the oil separates.
5. Now add the marinated chicken and sauté for 2–3 minutes. Add 1 cup water, saffron strands and cover the pan with a lid. Let simmer for 5–6 minutes on medium heat.
6. Add the yoghurt, cream, salt and mix well. Cook for 5 minutes. Check the seasoning and add water depending on the desired consistency of the gravy. Cook for 3–4 minutes on a low heat.
7. Once the chicken is cooked through, finish with the cardamom powder. Serve hot.

Bowl Assembly Serve the Chicken Korma with Saffron Pilaf (p. 52) and Kachumber (p. 30). You can also pair this with Buttered Govindobhog Rice (p. 51), or fresh Luchis (p. 45) and a salad of your choice.

Andhra Green Chilli Chicken

My go-to recipe for an easy, quick and delicious meal – this recipe has become a totem for shared laughter, sunlit afternoons and bonding over food. Don't be afraid to experiment – add more fresh chillies to give it a spicier kick or include sesame oil in the marinade to give a nutty flavour and aroma.

Cooking Time

30 mins

Serves

2

Ingredients

- ½ Tbsp Honey
- Lemon zest of 1 lemon
- Juice from 3 lemons
- 1 tsp Cumin seeds
- 1 Tbsp Soy sauce
- 2 tsp Garlic paste
- 2 tsp Vinegar
- ½ cup Finely chopped coriander leaves
- 2 Green chillies
- Salt, to taste
- 4 Chicken breasts or drumsticks
- 1 Tbsp Olive oil or any other cooking oil

Method

1. In a large bowl, add the honey, lemon zest, lemon juice, cumin seeds, soy sauce, garlic paste, vinegar, coriander leaves, green chillies, salt and mix well to create the marinade.
2. Add the chicken to the marinade and make sure it is evenly coated. Set aside in the refrigerator to marinate for a minimum of 2 hours.
3. Heat the oil in a heavy-bottomed pan on medium heat. Once the oil is hot, sear the chicken on each side for 2 minutes.
4. Add the leftover marinade to the pan, then cover the pan with a lid and cook on medium heat for another 3–4 minutes, until the chicken is fully cooked. If using drumsticks, cook for 15 minutes.

Bowl Assembly Serve Andhra Green Chilli Chicken with Ghee and Chilli Millet (p. 57), Purple Cabbage and Green Peas Salad (p. 29) along with Tomato Jaggery Chutney (p. 20).

MEAT Bowls

Chapli Kebab

Known for its distinct flat, round shape and the use of a mix of aromatic spices, this melt-in-your-mouth kebab with Pashtuni origins is a personal favourite! The subtle flavours of the dried pomegranate adds a beautiful tart flavour and helps to tenderize the meat.

Cooking Time

35 mins

Serves

4-6

Ingredients

- 500 gm Mutton mince
- 1 egg, beaten
- 1 Soft-boiled egg
- 1 Tomato, deseeded and finely chopped
- 1 Onion, finely chopped
- 3 tsp Dried pomegranate powder (anardana powder)
- 1 tsp Coriander powder
- 1 Tbsp Roasted cumin powder (p. 11)
- 1 tsp Red chilli powder
- 4 Tbsp Finely chopped coriander leaves
- Salt, to taste
- 3 Tbsp Cooking oil

Method

1. In a large bowl, add the mutton mince, beaten egg, boiled egg, tomato, onion, dried pomegranate powder, coriander powder, cumin powder, red chilli powder, coriander leaves and salt. Use your hands and mix well to combine. In case the kebab mixture turns too moist, add breadcrumbs or a boiled mashed potato to help absorb the excess moisture and prevent the kebabs from crumbling.
2. Lightly oil your hands and divide the meat mixture into lime-sized 10–12 portions. To create the kebab patties, press each meat ball down between your palms. This should produce ¼-inch thick kebabs.
3. Another method to shape the kebabs is to place the meatballs on top of a grease paper-lined plate, and press down with damp hands to shape the kebab patties. Don't worry about these kebabs being perfectly round, they are traditionally made with uneven edges.
4. Heat the oil in a non-stick pan over medium heat. Once the oil is hot, place the kebabs in small batches in the pan. Fry the kebabs for 5–6 minutes on each side. Serve hot.
5. Frozen, the raw kebabs can be stored up to 2 months, just defrost them 4–5 hours before cooking.

Bowl Assembly Add Kabuli Pulao (p. 53) in a bowl as the base. Place the Chapli Kebabs and add any salad greens to cut though the richness of the kebab. Pair with your favourite salad, or chopped/spiralized vegetables. You can also serve the kebabs on their own, paired with Green Garlic Chutney (p. 18) or Mint Yoghurt (p. 22).

Variation Swap the mutton with chicken mince. In step 3, fry the kebabs 4 minutes on each side on low heat.

Shami Kebab

Tender meat and lentil patties

The most popular kebabs from North India, they can be prepped ahead and frozen for up to a month.

Cooking Time

45 mins

Serves

4

Ingredients

FOR THE KEBAB:

- 500 gm Mutton mince
- 1 cup Split Bengal gram (chana dal)
- 1 Potato, quartered
- 1 Onion, quartered
- 6 Red chillies
- 2 Green chillies
- 1-inch Ginger piece, chopped
- 6 Garlic cloves
- 2 Black cardamoms
- 2 Cloves
- 1 tsp Cumin seeds
- 12 Whole black peppercorns
- ½ tsp Garam masala
- Salt, to taste
- 1 cup Water
- 1 Egg
- Cooking oil, for frying

FOR THE FILLING:

- 4 Onions, finely chopped
- 1-inch Ginger piece, finely chopped
- 3 Green chillies, finely chopped
- 1 Tbsp Chopped mint
- 1 tsp Lemon juice
- Salt, to taste
- 1 Gram flour (besan)

Method

1. Place a pan on medium heat and add the mutton mince, chana dal, potato, onion, red chillies, green chillies, ginger, garlic, cardamoms, cloves, cumin seeds, black peppercorns and salt along with 1 cup water. Cook for 20–30 minutes, until the meat is cooked and all the water has evaporated. Set aside to cool.
2. Once the mince is cool, dry grind it in a food processor on the lowest setting, scraping down the grinder jar whenever necessary. The paste should be uniform and well combined. Take care not to grind the meat too smooth, else the kebabs will lose their texture.
3. Place the kebab mix in a mixing bowl and add an egg. Mix well to combine.
4. To make the filling, in a separate bowl, add the onions, ginger, green chillies, chopped mint, lemon juice and salt. Mix well to combine.
5. Oil your hands and divide the kebab mix into 12–15 portions. Roll each portion in your palms, and put a little stuffing in the centre. Now shape them into small flat round cakes, patching up any cracks, if they appear. If you find that the kebab mix is too wet, then add 1 Tbsp gram flour (if needed).
6. To set the kebabs, chill them in the fridge for 10 minutes.
7. Heat the oil in a pan on low heat. Once the oil is hot, but not smoking, shallow fry the kebabs lightly for 4–5 minutes on each side, until a golden crust appears.

Bowl Assembly Serve the Shami Kebab with Saffron Pilaf (p. 52) and Kala Channa Chat (p. 32). Or enjoy this with Masala Onions (p. 28) and Mint Yoghurt (p. 22). These kebabs also work well as filling for wraps or sandwiches. Place a kebab or two with slices of tomatoes, cucumbers and onions and a dollop of a chutney of your choice. I also crumble these kebabs and add them to my salads!

Quick tip The best cut for these kebabs is the pasanda, which are boneless chunks from the hind leg of baby lamb/goat.

30-Minute Mutton Biryani

The ultimate comfort food for so many people across the country, with every state having its own signature style – mutton biryani does not need any introduction. I have created a simplified recipe without compromising on the flavour.

Cooking Time

30 mins

Serves

6

Ingredients

- 1 kg Basmati rice
- 1 kg Mutton, curry cut
- ½ cup Ginger-garlic paste (p. 9)
- 1 tsp Turmeric
- Salt, to taste
- 500 gm Yoghurt
- 150 ml Ghee
- 12 Green cardamoms (divided)
- 2 tsp Cumin seeds (divided)
- 14 cups Water (divided)
- 4 Cloves
- 1 Two-inch Cinnamon stick
- 2 tsp Red chilli powder
- Birista of two large onions (p. 10)
- 10 sprigs Coriander leaves, chopped
- 25–30 Mint leaves
- 6 Green chillies, slit lengthwise
- 8–10 Saffron strands dissolved in ½ cup milk

Method

1. Wash and soak the rice for 30 minutes in cold water. Drain and set aside.
2. Combine the mutton pieces with ginger-garlic paste, turmeric, 2 tsp salt and yoghurt. Marinate overnight, if possible or for a minimum of 2 hours.
3. Heat the ghee in a handi or a large, deep pot on medium-high heat. Once the ghee is hot, turn the heat to low and add 6 cardamoms, 1 tsp cumin seeds. Fry for 1 minute, until the cumin smells fragrant. Add the mutton and sauté for 5 minutes. Add 2 cups water and cover the pan with a lid. Cook for 30 minutes.
4. Meanwhile in another large pan over medium heat, put 12 cups water to boil with cloves, salt, cinnamon, 6 cardamoms and 1 tsp cumin seeds. Once the water comes to a boil, add the rice and cook until it's ¾ parts done. This will take 8–9 minutes. Drain the rice through a strainer and keep aside.
5. Check if the mutton is done by piercing it with a fork. The mutton should be tender, allowing the fork to go through it easily. If the mutton remains uncooked, add 1 cup water, then cover and cook.
6. Once the meat is cooked, add the chilli powder and cook for 5 minutes.
7. To assemble the biryani, in a large, deep-bottomed pot or handi, place a layer of the cooked rice. Top it with a portion of the mutton, birista, coriander leaves, mint leaves and green chillies. Repeat this process – the top layer should be rice. Pour the saffron milk over the rice.
8. Cover the pot with aluminum foil. Cover with a lid and place a heavy object on top to further secure the lid. Cook for 15 minutes on low heat. Remove from heat and serve.

Bowl Assembly Serve the Mutton Biryani with a side of Burani Raita (p. 22). You can also serve this with a side of Kachumber (p. 30) and Mirchi Ka Salan (p. 41).

Masala Lamb Chops

When picking lamb chops at the store, look for chops that are pink to red with white marbling. For this recipe, ribs work best.

Cooking Time

45 mins

Serves

4

Ingredients

8 pcs	Lamb chops
2 Tbsp	Cooking oil
2 tsp	Red chilli powder
1 tsp	Cumin powder
½ tsp	Garam masala
5 tsp	Ginger-garlic paste (p. 9)
2 cups	Hung yoghurt (p. 11)
	Juice from 2 lemons.
½ tsp	Dried fenugreek leaves (kasuri methi)
	Salt, to taste

Method

1. Ensure that lamb chops are dry, wipe off any moisture using a paper towel. Pound the thicker part of the lamb till it is about half the thickness.
2. In a large bowl, add the cooking oil, red chilli powder, cumin powder, garam masala, ginger-garlic paste, hung yoghurt, lemon juice and fenugreek leaves. Whisk together until smooth. Add the lamb chops and mix well, to ensure that the marinade coats the chops evenly.
3. Cover the bowl and leave to marinate for a minimum of 2 hours, or prep ahead and marinate them overnight. Remove the lamb chops from the fridge 30 minutes before cooking.
4. Preheat oven to 200 degrees C.
5. Place a cast iron pan or a heavy-bottomed pan that can be used in an oven over high heat. Once the pan is hot, add 4 lamb chops at a time and sear for 5–6 minutes on each side until they are browned on the outside with some crusty bits. Using tongs press the chops down so that the fat renders and turns crisp and brown. This prevents the lamb chops from being overcooked while the fat renders.
6. Remove from heat, and place the pan into the oven and cook for 4–5 minutes, on each side.

Quick tip To reheat these lamb chops without losing moisture, bake them for 5–10 minutes on each side in a 200 degree C oven, covered with aluminum foil. One can also add in a splash of stock or butter to keep the lamb chop moist while reheating. If reheating in a microwave, put the chops in a microwave safe bowl with a splash of water or stock and heat for 3 minutes.

Bowl Assembly I have served the Masala Lamb Chops on a bed of pumpkin chokha, you can serve them with Aloo Chokha (p. 72) or any vegetable mash of your choice. Pair with a side of Sprouts Kachumber (p. 30).

Nalli Gosht

Lamb shanks slow cooked in a rich, flavourful gravy

I have spent several winter mornings at Old Delhi eateries, that serve Nalli Gosht for breakfast at 7 a.m. Try this recipe to recreate the magic of those cold, winter mornings in your kitchen.

Cooking Time

1 hr 30 mins

Serves

4

Ingredients

2 Tbsp Cooking oil
2 Onions (divided), 1 finely chopped and 1 thinly sliced
25 Garlic cloves
½ cup Ghee
8 Green cardamoms
3 Cinnamon sticks
3 Cloves
2 Bay leaves
4 Tbsp Ginger-garlic paste (p.9)
1 kg Lamb shanks
Salt, to taste
1 tsp Turmeric
3 tsp Kashmiri red chilli powder mixed with 1 Tbsp water
250 gm Whisked yoghurt
500 ml Water
½ tsp Garam masala
½ tsp Green cardamom powder
2 tsp Pandanus water (Kewra water)
2 tsp Rose water
1 gm Saffron strands
½ tsp Black pepper powder

TO GARNISH

Ginger juliennes
Coriander leaves, finely chopped

Method

1. Heat 1 Tbsp oil in a pan on medium-high heat. Once the oil is hot, turn the heat to low and add the chopped onion. Fry for 5–6 minutes on high heat, continuously stirring until golden brown. Remove with a slotted spoon and set aside.
2. In the same pan, add the remaining oil on medium-high heat. Once the oil is hot, turn the heat to low, add the garlic cloves and fry for 5–6 minutes, until they are brown. Remove and set aside.
3. Place the fried onions and garlic, along with 3 tsp water in a food processor and blitz to a smooth paste.
4. Heat the ghee in a pan on medium-high heat. Once the ghee is hot, turn the heat down to low and add the cardamoms, cinnamon sticks, cloves and bay leaves and fry for 1 minute, until fragrant.
5. Add the sliced onions and fry for 5-6 minutes, until golden brown. Add the ginger-garlic paste and lamb shanks. Sauté for 1 minute – add salt, turmeric and red chilli paste, and sauté for 5 minutes.
6. Add the garlic and onion paste, yoghurt and mix well. Cover and cook on low heat for 15 minutes. Pour in the water and cover and cook till the mutton is cooked, and falling off the bone. This will take 30–40 minutes.
7. Add the garam masala, cardamom powder, kewra water, rose water, saffron and black pepper powder. Mix well, and cook for 10 minutes. Serve hot, garnished with ginger and coriander leaves.

Bowl Assembly Pair the Nalli Gosht with Ghee and Chilli Millet (p. 57), Sprouts Kachumber (p. 30) and Masala Onions (p. 28). You can also enjoy this with a bread of your choice, or serve it with Kabuli Pulao (p. 53) and a fresh salad.

Tabak Maaz

Fried lamb ribs

This traditional Kashmiri dish is easy to make and can be served as a starter by itself, or as part of a meal. For best results, pick ribs with fat on them.

Cooking Time

1 hr 15 mins

Serves

4

Ingredients

4 litres	Water (divided), 2 litres at room temperature and 2 litres cold
1 kg	Mutton ribs
4½ tsp	Garlic paste
5½ tsp	Salt
2 tsp	Dried ginger powder
8	Cloves
8	Black cardamoms
3½ tsp	Turmeric
2½ cups	Ghee

Method

1. Place a heavy-bottomed vessel on high heat. Pour in 2 litres of water, and bring to a boil. The water should be enough to just cover the ribs. Turn the heat down to medium-high and add the ribs.
2. Bring to a boil, and remove the scum that rises to the surface. Repeat until the water is clear. Cover and continue to boil the ribs for 20 minutes, until half done.
3. Add the garlic paste and boil for another 10 minutes. Add 3½ tsp salt, then cover and boil for 10 minutes.
4. Take the pan off the heat, remove the ribs and set aside to cool. Discard the water.
5. Once the ribs reach room temperature, immerse them in 2 litres of cold water. Wash thoroughly and set aside. Do not discard the water.
6. Place a heavy-bottomed vessel on high heat. Pour in the water in which the ribs were washed and bring to a boil.
7. Turn the heat to low and add the ribs, 2 tsp salt, ginger powder, cloves, black cardamoms and turmeric. Stir and boil for 15 minutes, until the ribs are fully cooked. To check if the ribs are done, pierce the membrane between them with your thumb. If the membrane yields easily, the ribs are cooked through.
8. Remove the pan from heat and take out the ribs with a slotted spoon. Set aside and discard the water.
9. Heat the ghee in a pan over medium-high heat.
10. In another large frying pan, arrange the ribs in a manner in which they don't overlap. Now, place the pan over low heat.
11. Once the ghee is hot (step 9) pour over the ribs. Fry the ribs, turning them at intervals, until they turn reddish brown all over. Drain the ghee before serving.

Bowl Assembly Pair the Tabak Maaz with Saffron Pilaf (p. 52) and Saag (p. 45). Serve with a side of Doon Chetin (p. 20).

Highway Mutton Curry

This is a family recipe, passed on to me by my uncle who ran a dhabha in pre-partition India. It is hearty, warm and comforting. The recipe works just as well with chicken.

Cooking Time

40 mins

Serves

4

Ingredients

- 125 gm Ghee
- 1 Three-inch cinnamon stick
- 4 Cloves
- 1 Black cardamom
- 6 Green cardamoms
- 1 Bay leaf
- 1 tsp Garlic paste
- 1 tsp Ginger paste
- 500 gm Mutton, curry cut
- 1 Tbsp Yoghurt
- ½ tsp Tumeric
- Salt, to taste
- 1½ tsp Coriander powder
- 1 tsp Red chilli powder
- 1 Green chilli, sliced
- 3 Onions, fried and made into a paste (p. 9)
- 1 tsp Garam masala
- 1 tsp Pandanus water (Kewra water)

Method

1. Heat the ghee in a heavy-bottomed pan on medium-high heat. Once the ghee is hot, turn the heat to low and add the cinnamon, cloves, black cardamom and green cardamoms. Fry for 30 seconds, until the spices are fragrant. Add the ginger and garlic pastes and fry for 2 minutes, until the raw smell goes away.
2. Add the mutton pieces, tumeric and yoghurt and fry for 5 minutes. Add salt and mix well to combine.
3. Add the coriander and red chilli powder, green chilli and fried onion paste. Stir well and fry for 1 minute on medium heat.
4. Add enough water to just cover the meat. Cover with a lid and cook for 25 minutes on low-medium heat, until the meat is tender. If pressed for time, pressure cook the mutton for 3 whistles. If using chicken then skip using the pressure cooker.
5. Open the cooker and add the garam masala and kewra water. Let it simmer for 5–7 minutes and remove from heat.
6. If using chicken, in step 4 cover and cook the chicken for 25 minutes, until it is tender. Remove the lid, add the garam masala and kewra water. Let it simmer for 5 minutes and remove from heat.

Bowl Assembly Serve the Highway Mutton Curry with Peas Pulao (p. 53) and Jeera Aloo (p. 42). You can also pair this with Cumin Rice (p. 52), Koshimbir (p. 29) and Pickled Baby Onions (p. 28).

Aab Gosht

Kashmiri mutton curry

The ultimate in Kashmiri formal feasts, a wazwan traditionally consists of 36 dishes. Among the seven dishes which are a must at these occasions is Aab Gosht. Made without using chillies, ginger or garlic this fragrant and delicate curry has a watery consistency – *aab* means water in Persian – with just a hint of sweetness.

Cooking Time

60 mins

Serves

4

Ingredients

- 4 Tbsp Ghee
- 2 Medium-sized onions, ground to a paste
- 1 litre Water
- 800 gm Mutton chops or curry cut mutton
- Salt, to taste
- 1 Bay leaf
- 2 Cloves (divided)
- 12 Green cardamoms (divided)
- 2 Two-inch cinnamon sticks (divided)
- 1 litre Milk
- 10 Saffron strands
- ½ cup Cream
- ⅕ tsp Fennel powder
- ¼ tsp Cumin powder
- ¼ tsp Black pepper powder

Method

1. Heat 2 Tbsp ghee in a heavy-bottomed pan on medium-high heat. Once the oil is hot, but not smoking, turn the heat to low and add the onion paste. Fry for 5–6 minutes, until golden brown. Remove from heat and set aside.
2. Place a large pan on medium-high heat. Add 1 litre water, followed by the mutton, salt, bay leaf, 1 clove, 6 cardamoms, 1 cinnamon stick and the fried onion paste and bring to a boil. Turn the heat to low and continue to boil for 30 minutes, or until the meat is tender. Once it is done, strain the meat and save the stock.
3. While the meat is cooking, bring the milk to a boil in another pan with the remaining cloves, cardamoms and cinnamon. Turn the heat to low and let simmer, stirring till the milk reduces to a third. This will take about 40 minutes. Once the milk is done, add the saffron strands. Remove from heat and set aside to cool.
4. Once the milk reaches room temperature, add in the cream and mix well. Now add the meat and 500 ml stock (step 2) to the milk and put back on the stove on low heat.
5. In another pan, heat 2 Tbsp ghee on medium heat. Once the ghee is hot, turn the heat to low and add fennel powder and fry briefly for 10 seconds. Add the cumin powder and black pepper powder and cook for 10 seconds. Do this quickly, to ensure that the spice powders don't burn.
6. Pour the spice temper into the curry and cook the curry for another 5 minutes and serve hot.

Bowl Assembly I like to serve the Aab Gosht with Manipuri Black Rice (p. 51), Carrot Thoran (p. 35) and Saag (p. 45).

Mutton Kofta

Spiced meatballs

These delicious mutton koftas can be served as a snack with a chutney or dip, but are also great eaten in a wrap, or crumbled on top of a salad.

Cooking Time

45 mins

Serves

4

Ingredients

- 500 gm Mutton mince
- 3 Tbsp Cooking oil (divided)
- 1 Large egg
- 10 Garlic cloves, finely chopped
- 1 tsp Cumin powder
- 1 tsp Coriander powder
- 1 tsp Smoked paprika
- Salt, to taste
- ½ tsp Black pepper powder
- 2 Tbsp Water

Method

1. Place the mutton mince, 1 Tbsp oil, egg, garlic, cumin powder, coriander powder, paprika, salt and pepper in a food processor and blitz to a smooth paste.
2. Oil your hands and shape the ground meat into 18–20 golf ball-sized koftas.
3. Heat the remaining 2 Tbsp cooking oil in a pan on high heat. Once the oil is hot but not smoking, reduce the heat to medium and add the koftas. Sauté for 4–5 minutes, until the koftas are brown on all sides.
4. Turn the heat to low, and add 2 Tbsp water, cover and cook the koftas for 8–10 minutes. To check if the koftas are cooked through, break 1 in the middle and check if they are done. If they are still uncooked, cover and cook for another 5 minutes.
5. Once shaped, place the koftas on a parchment-lined plate and freeze until solid. Once frozen, pop them into a freezable bag and store for up to 2 weeks.

Bowl Assembly Serve the Mutton Koftas with Tomato Quinoa (p. 54), Lehsun Mirchi Chutney (p. 19) and toasted kulchas. The koftas also pair well with Coconut Millet (p. 57), and Mint Yoghurt (p. 22).

Mutton Keema

Minced mutton cooked with peas

This easy, one-pot meal is a much-loved Indian dish. Eat with warm bread or kulchas.

Cooking Time

40 mins

Serves

4

Ingredients

- 2 Tbsp Cooking oil
- 8 Black peppercorns
- 2 Cloves
- 1 Black cardamom
- 1 tsp Cumin seeds
- 1 Bay leaf
- 1 Onion, finely chopped
- 1 tsp Ginger paste
- 1 tsp Garlic paste
- 2 Tomatoes, finely chopped
- 1 Tbsp Water
- ¼ tsp Turmeric
- 1 tsp Red chilli powder
- 1 tsp Coriander powder
- ½ tsp Cumin powder
- Salt, to taste
- 500 gm Mutton mince
- 100 gm Green peas, boiled (p. 29)
- 1 Tbsp Chopped coriander

Method

1. Heat the oil in a saucepan over medium heat. Once the oil is hot, add the peppercorns, cloves, black cardamom, cumin seeds and bay leaf. Fry for 30 seconds, until the spices smell fragrant.
2. Add the onions and fry for 4–5 minutes, until light brown.
3. Add the ginger and garlic pastes and cook for 1–2 minutes. Add the chopped tomatoes, 1 Tbsp water and cook for 7–8 minutes until the tomatoes are soft and the oil separates.
4. Add the turmeric, red chilli powder, coriander powder, cumin powder, salt and the mutton mince. Cook for 7–8 minutes, stirring constantly until all the moisture has evaporated. Keep separating the mutton with the back of the ladle to ensure it does not clump together.
5. Now, add the peas and cover the saucepan. Cook over medium heat for 5–7 minutes, until the meat is cooked through and dry. Garnish with coriander and remove from heat. Serve hot.

Bowl Assembly Serve the Mutton Keema with pav or any bread of your choice, Pudina Dhania Chutney (p. 18), raw onions, a fried green chilli and lemon wedges. You can pair the Mutton Keema with a grain or eat on its own, with a salad of your choice.

Raw Mango and Keema Rice

Easy and quick to put together, the addition of raw mangoes to the keema lends the dish a fresh, sour punch.

Cooking Time

20 mins

Serves

4

Ingredients

- 3 Medium-sized raw mangoes (divided)
- 2 Tbsp Ghee
- 2 Green chillies, chopped
- ¼ tsp Turmeric
- ½ tsp Red chilli powder
- 1 tsp Dried mango powder (amchur)
- 350 gm Cooked mutton keema (p. 180)
- 500 gm Cooked basmati rice (p. 50)
- ½ cup Water
- Salt, to taste

Method

1. Peel and deseed 1 mango. Cut into rough chunks and add to a food processor with 1 Tbsp water and blitz to a smooth paste.
2. Peel and deseed the remaining 2 mangoes. Chop them into small dices and set aside.
3. Heat the ghee in a deep-bottomed pan on medium heat. Once the ghee is hot, add the chillies and sauté for 30 seconds.
4. Add the raw mango paste, tumeric, red chilli powder and dried mango powder. Sauté for 1 minute on low heat and add 1 Tbsp water.
5. Add the keema and sauté for 3–4 minutes on medium heat.
6. Add the rice with ½ cup water and gently mix it with the keema. Add the chopped raw mangoes and salt. Cover and cook on a low heat for 5 minutes. Serve hot.

Bowl Assembly Serve the Raw Mango and Keema Rice in a bowl with Kachumber (p. 30) and a dollop of Aam Ki Launji (p. 17). Or eat this with a serving of Beetroot Yoghurt (p. 23) and Kurkuri Bhindi (p. 39) or Mustard Baby Potatoes (p. 43).

Sausage Tawa Masala

Griddle-fried sausages in a spicy masala

This is a easy take on the famous tawa (griddle) masala meat dishes of North India.

Cooking Time

30 mins

Serves

4

Ingredients

FOR THE ONION-TOMATO MASALA

1½ Tbsp Cooking oil
1 Bay leaf
2 tsp Cumin seeds
1 cup Chopped onion
1 Tbsp Chopped garlic
2 Green Chillies
1 Tbsp Chopped ginger
½ tsp Turmeric
1 tsp Red chilli powder
½ tsp Coriander powder
Salt, to taste
2 Tbsp Water
2 cups Chopped tomato

FOR THE SAUSAGE TAWA MASALA

½ Tbsp Cooking oil
6 Garlic cloves, chopped
6 Dried red chillies
12 Pork sausages, sliced into 1-inch pieces
1 Red bell pepper, sliced into strips
1 Yellow bell pepper, sliced into strips
1 Capsicum, sliced into strips
2 Tbsp Roasted coriander powder (p. 10)
2 Tbsp Onion-tomato masala
Salt, to taste
2tsp Lemon juice

Method

1. To make the onion-tomato masala, heat the oil in a pan on medium heat. Add the bay leaf and cumin seeds and sauté for 1 minute.
2. Add the onion and stir-fry for 5–7 minutes, until brown. Add the garlic, green chillies and ginger and sauté for 1 minute. Add the turmeric, red chilli powder, coriander powder, salt along with 1 Tbsp water and sauté for 1 minute.
3. Add the tomatoes and cook on medium heat. You will know it is done, when the tomatoes turn mushy and the oil separates.
4. Add 1 Tbsp water, cover the pan with a lid and cook on low heat for 5 minutes. Remove from heat.
5. To make the sausage tawa masala, in another pan heat the oil on medium-high heat. Once the oil is hot, turn the heat to low and add the chopped garlic and whole red chillies. Sauté for 2–3 minutes, until the garlic turns translucent.
6. Add the sausages and sauté for 2 minutes. Add the red, yellow and green bell peppers and roasted coriander powder. Sauté on medium heat for 3 minutes.
7. Add the onion-tomato masala, season with salt and sauté for another 3 minutes. Turn off the heat. Add the lime juice and mix. Serve hot.

Bowl Assembly Serve with a side of toasted bread or kulcha and Lentil Salad (p. 31). You can also pair the Sausage Tawa Masala with Khichdi with Garlic Tadka (p. 55) or eat it on its own, along with a salad of your choice.

Seekh Masala Fry

A quick and easy recipe using store bought frozen seekh kebabs, this one is handy for the nights when all you want is a fuss-free dinner.

Cooking Time

20 mins

Serves

4

Ingredients

- 8 Mutton or chicken seekh kebabs, cut into ½-inch pieces (I used mutton kebabs)
- 1 Tbsp Cooking oil
- 2 tsp Ginger-garlic paste (p.9)
- ½ tsp Cumin powder
- 1 tsp Red chilli powder
- 1½ Tbsp Water (divided)
- 2 Tomatoes, roughly chopped
- 2 Green chillies, chopped
- 2 Medium-sized onions, sliced
- Juice from 1 lemon

Method

1. Thaw the frozen seekh kebabs in the refrigerator for about 4 hours or at room temperature for 30 minutes before cooking.
2. Heat the oil in a pan on medium-high heat. Once the oil is hot, turn the heat to low and add the ginger-garlic paste and sauté for 1 minute till fragrant.
3. Add the cumin powder, red chilli powder and ½ Tbsp water and sauté for 30 seconds. Add the kebabs and sauté on low heat for 3–4 minutes, till the kebabs are cooked.
4. Add the tomatoes and green chillies and sauté for 3–4 minutes on low heat. Add the onions and sauté for 2–3 minutes, till the onions become translucent.
5. Add 1 Tbsp water and cover and cook on low heat for another 2 minutes. Remove from heat and add the lemon juice. Serve hot.
6. This recipe can also be tossed with some leftover rice to make a quick, delicious rice bowl. Just add a portion of cooked rice after step 4, and mix well to combine.

Bowl assembly Serve the Seekh Masala Fry with Khichdi with Garlic Tadka (p. 55) and Avocado Kachumber (p. 30). You can also add Pudina Dhania Chutney (p. 18) some Masala Onions (p. 28) and lettuce to a paratha and make yourself a delicious kathi roll.

DESSERT
Bowls

Bhapa Doi with Figs

Baked yoghurt with figs and panjiri crumble

The baked yoghurt can be served on its own, but do also make the fully-fledged dessert with all the accompaniments.

Cooking Time

60 mins

Serves

4

Ingredients

FOR THE BAKED YOGHURT

- ½ cup Yoghurt
- ½ cup Heavy cream
- ½ cup Condensed milk
- ½ tsp Vanilla essence
- 4 Dried figs

FOR THE CHERRY COMPOTE

- 2 cups Pitted cherries or any frozen berries of your choice
- 1 Star anise
- ½ Tbsp Sugar
- 1 tsp Vanilla essence

FOR THE PANJIRI

- 1½ cup Ghee (divided)
- ½ cup Edible gum crystals (gond)
- ½ cup Slivered almonds
- ½ cup Sliced cashews
- 8 Walnuts, chopped
- 2 cups Wholewheat flour
- 1 cup Powdered jaggery
- ½ tsp Cardamom powder

Method

1. To make the baked yoghurt, preheat oven to 120 degrees C. Set up a baking tray with high edges, and fill it halfway with water and place it in the oven.
2. In a bowl add the yoghurt, cream, condensed milk and vanilla essence. Using a whisk, mix well until smooth and the mixture has no lumps.
3. Pour equal amounts of the yoghurt mixture in 4 ramekins. Now place a dried fig in each ramekin.
4. Place the ramekins in the baking tray with water and bake for 15 minutes, or until the top sets and the centre turns jiggly. If it is still runny, bake for another 3–4 minutes. Remove the ramekins from the oven and allow to cool to room temperature. Refrigerate for 6–8 hours.
5. To make the cherry compote, place the cherries and star anise in a small saucepan and cook on medium heat.
6. Once the cherries start bubbling, reduce heat to low. Use a wooden spoon to roughly mash the cherries.
7. Add the sugar and vanilla essence and continue cooking over low-medium heat for 10–12 minutes. Remove from heat, cool and refrigerate for a minimum of 1 hour.
8. To make the panjiri, heat 1 Tbsp ghee in a heavy-bottomed pan. Add the gond and sauté for 4–5 minutes on medium heat, until it puffs up and doubles in size. Remove from the pan and allow it to cool completely.
9. Grind the gond in a blender until it reaches a coarse texture. Set aside.
10. Heat 1 Tbsp ghee in a pan. Add the almonds, cashews and walnuts. Sauté for 2–3 minutes. Set aside in a bowl.
11. Add 1 cup ghee to the same pan over medium heat. Once the ghee is hot, add the wholewheat flour and cook, stirring constantly for 20–25 minutes, or until golden brown. Remove from heat and transfer to a mixing bowl.
12. While the flour is hot, add the jaggery and mix well using a spoon. Next, toss in the toasted nuts, cardamom powder and crushed gond and mix well.

Bowl Assembly Take the set yoghurt and pour a spoonful of the cherry compote on it. Sprinkle 1 Tbsp panjiri around the cherry compote and serve.

Sheer Khurma

Vermicelli milk pudding

Sheer Khurma is a festive favourite – an Eid morning must. This can be served hot or cold, and the consistency can be drinkable or thick – it's a forgiving recipe. The sesame chikki or brittle is a nutritious treat and can be made ahead.

Cooking Time

60 mins

Serves

4

Ingredients

FOR THE SHEER KHURMA

- 5 Tbsp Ghee
- 150 gm Vermicelli
- 1½ litre Milk
- 100 gm Sugar
- ½ tin Condensed milk
- 10 Dates, sliced
- 10–15 Raisins, chopped
- 20–25 Pistachios, chopped
- 25–30 Almonds, sliced
- A few saffron strands

FOR THE SESAME CHIKKI

- 1½ cup Sugar
- 3 Tbsp Water
- ½ cup White sesame seeds
- ½ cup Black sesame seeds

Method

1. Place the ghee in a heavy-bottomed pan on high heat. Once the ghee is hot, add the vermicelli and fry until it turns golden brown.
2. Add the milk and sugar and bring to a slow boil. This should take 4–5 minutes.
3. Add the condensed milk, dates and raisins. Allow the mixture to thicken on a low heat for about 15 minutes.
4. Remove from the pan and set aside. Garnish with the chopped pistachios, sliced almonds and saffron strands.
5. To make the sesame chikki, line a large baking sheet with parchment paper or a silpat mat.
6. Combine the sugar and water in a small saucepan over medium heat. Stir until the sugar is uniformly mixed. Then cook undisturbed for 6–8 minutes, until the mixture bubbles steadily and turns golden brown.
7. Switch off the stove and slowly stir in the white and black sesame seeds.
8. Immediately pour the mixture on the prepared baking sheet. Using an oiled metal spatula, quickly spread the mixture to a thin even layer. Cool for 30 minutes at room temperature. Tap gently with a ladle or knife to break the brittle into pieces.
9. Store the brittle in an airtight container. It lasts up to a month at room temperature.

Bowl Assembly For one portion, scoop out a generous portion of the sheer khurma in a bowl and top generously with the sesame chikki.

Brûléed Phirni

If you are looking for a dinner party dish with a degree of flair, this brûléed Indian rice pudding dessert ticks the box. All elements can be made ahead and assembled at the last minute. Phirni can be served on its own, but the compote adds a nice tart note to it. And it is quite a multitasking condiment – swirl it into yoghurt, add a dollop to oatmeal or ice-cream, or eat it on toast. If strawberries are not in season, frozen ones work just as well.

Cooking Time

60 mins

Serves

4

Ingredients

FOR THE PHIRNI

- 50 gm Basmati rice
- 1 litre Full fat milk
- 150 gm Sugar
- 1 tsp Green cardamom powder
- 1 tsp Saffron strands
- 2 tsp Rose water
- 2 Tbsp Castor sugar, to brûlée

FOR THE STRAWBERRY COMPOTE

- 2 cups Strawberries, cut into half
- 1 Three-inch cinnamon stick
- 1 Tbsp Sugar
- 1 tsp Vanilla essence

Method

1. To make the phirni, wash the rice and soak in water for 30 minutes. Strain the rice using a colander and transfer to a food processor. Grind the rice to a paste. This should take 4–5 short pulses. The rice paste should not be coarse or too fine.
2. In a wok over high heat bring the milk to a boil. Reduce the heat and add the ground rice. Stir immediately to stop the rice from clumping. Stir continuously – this will ensure that your pudding doesn't catch at the bottom – let it reduce for 30 minutes.
3. At this stage the rice will be almost done and the milk should have thickened into a pudding-like consistency.
4. Add the sugar and cardamom powder, and continue stirring for 2–3 minutes. Then add the saffron strands and keep stirring for another minute. Turn off the heat and add the rose water. Pour the phirni into 4 serving bowls and let it cool for 30 minutes.
5. Cover the phirni bowls with cling film to avoid the top of the pudding running dry. To set the phirni, refrigerate for a minimum of 2 hours. The phirni will keep well in the fridge for 3 days.
6. To make the strawberry compote, place the strawberries and cinnamon in a small saucepan over medium heat. Once the strawberries start bubbling, reduce the heat to low. Using a wooden spoon, mash the strawberries at regular intervals.
7. Add the sugar and vanilla essence and continue cooking over medium-low heat for 10–12 minutes. Remove from heat and transfer to a clean container to cool. Refrigerate once it reaches room temperature. The compote will keep for 1 week in the fridge.

Bowl Assembly Just before serving, sprinkle the castor sugar on the phirni and using a culinary torch, melt the sugar to form a crispy, crunchy sugar coating. Allow this to harden for a minute. Top with the compote and serve.

Saffron and Cardamom Spiced Tea Cake

This light tea cake is a great companion to evening tea, but works just as well as a dessert option. The custard cream is also delicious spooned over fruits or eaten sprinkled with nuts.

Cooking Time

60 mins

Serves

4

Ingredients

FOR THE CAKE

- 8-10 Saffron threads
- 255 gm All-purpose flour (maida)
- 2 tsp Baking powder
- 1¼ tsp Cardamom powder
- ½ tsp Salt
- Butter for greasing the baking dish
- Flour for dusting the baking dish
- 4 Tbsp Unsalted butter, at room temperature
- 300 gm Sugar
- 4 Eggs
- 180 ml Milk
- ½ cup Cooking oil
- 1 tsp Vanilla essence

FOR THE CUSTARD CREAM

- 250 ml Milk
- 4 Egg yolks
- 70 gm Castor sugar
- 30 gm All-purpose flour (maida)
- 500 gm Whipped cream

Method

1. Preheat oven to 180 degrees C.
2. To make the tea cake, soak the saffron threads in 1 Tbsp hot water for 5 minutes.
3. Sift together the flour, baking powder, cardamom and salt in a bowl and set aside.
4. Butter and flour a cake pan. I used a loaf mould but you can use a cake pan, 8–9 inches in size.
5. Using a fork, lightly beat the butter and sugar in a large bowl for 3–4 minutes, until it is well-blended, fluffy and pale yellow. Add the eggs one at a time, beat until the egg is incorporated and then add another. Repeat the process till all the eggs have been incorporated and the butter is light and fluffy.
6. Beat in the milk, oil, vanilla and saffron. I used an electric mixer on medium speed, you can also whisk by hand. This will take 5 minutes.
7. Gently fold in half of the prepared flour into the milk and eggs mixture. Once the mix looks well combined, add in the rest of the flour and mix. Make sure not to over-mix.
8. Pour the batter into the prepared pan and bake for 35 minutes till golden. To check if the cake is done, insert a toothpick and if it comes out clean, it is ready.
9. Remove from the oven and then gently demould the cake – take a butter knife and gently loosen the edges of the cake from the pan, put a plate on top of the cake tin and flip to demould. Let it rest.
10. To make the custard cream, in a pan boil the milk and set aside till it reaches room temperature.
11. In a large bowl, beat the egg yolks and sugar for 2–3 minutes.
12. Whisk in the flour. Slowly pour the milk into the egg mixture and whisk to combine.
13. Place this mixture in a pan and cook over low heat until it thickens, about 10 minutes. Keep stirring continuously to ensure that the custard cream doesn't bubble. Keep aside and cover with cling film to prevent skin from forming.
14. Once cool, remove the cling film and mix in the whipped cream. This cream keeps well in the refrigerator for 3 days.

Bowl Assembly Slice a generous portion of the tea cake, top with custard cream and fresh seasonal fruits.

Spiced Dark Chocolate Mousse

This delicious and easy recipe is my go-to when all I want is chocolate. You can garnish this with strawberries or any fresh berries of your choice.

Cooking Time

30 mins

Serves

4

Ingredients

250 ml Milk
¼ tsp Cinnamon powder
¼ tsp Green cardamom powder
¼ tsp Black pepper powder
5 Egg yolks
40 gm Sugar
1 tsp Vanilla essence
Zest of 1 orange
500 gm Regular or cooking dark chocolate, chopped
300 gm Whipped cream, chilled

FOR THE GARNISH

200 gm Pitted cherries
2 Tbsp Whipped cream

Method

1. Place a medium-sized saucepan on medium heat, and pour enough water to cover 2 inches of the pan. Bring the water to a simmer and reduce the heat.
2. In a heatproof bowl, add the milk, cinnamon powder, cardamom powder, black pepper powder, egg yolks, sugar and vanilla essence.
3. Place the bowl atop the saucepan with hot water (step 1). The bowl should fit snuggly, and the bottom should not touch the water. If it dips into the water, it will be too hot.
4. Keep stirring the custard on low heat, until it thickens and coats the back of a spoon. This will take 12–15 minutes. Add the orange zest and mix.
5. In a separate bowl, place the chocolate and strain the custard over it. Stir until the chocolate melts completely. Keep aside and cool.
6. Once the chocolate mixture has reached room temperature, fold in the whipped cream and mix well to combine.
7. Pour the mixture into 4 serving bowls and refrigerate for a minimum of 2 hours.

Bowl Assembly Once the mousse is set, garnish with the pitted cherries and whipped cream and serve.

Acknowledgements

I would like to begin by thanking my editor, Priya Kapoor, who believed in me and entrusted me with her unique concept of presenting Indian food in a bowl. Her clear vision, thoughtful suggestions, and the tireless efforts of the team at Roli Books have shaped this book into what it is today.

My heartfelt thanks to the brilliant Anshika Varma, my photographer – and elder sister – who has captured the essence of this book in every frame. From guiding me through my first book to styling each bowl with such elegance, I am in awe of her talent, vision and unwavering support.

I will forever be grateful to my mother, Aditti Kohli, who manifested this dream for me – long before I could see it myself. She has been my first teacher, both in the kitchen and in life. Through her, I learned what it means to create meals that are not just delicious and nourishing, but also imaginative. She generously shared so many of her recipes for this book.

I would also like to thank the rest of my family – my father, Dhiraj, my brother Maddhav, Disha and Noah – for being my anchors. Their love and belief in me have meant everything.

A special and heartfelt thank you to Naorem Anuja. This book would not be what it is without her patience, sharp eye and dedication. She reviewed every recipe, endured my chaotic chef-style writing and poured countless hours into refining every detail.

Thank you to Joy Sir for generously opening the doors of Mezze Mambo for the shoot and for his constant encouragement. I am deeply grateful for his support.

A huge thank you to Shridula Chatterjee – words truly fall short. From recipes to shoots, edits to prep, she was there through it all. She made this journey lighter. This book is as much hers as it is mine.

While it's not possible to name every single person who played a role in bringing this book to life, I extend my deepest thanks to all who contributed in ways big and small. Their efforts, combined with the stories and recipes in these pages, are a testament to the love, passion and dedication that go into creating a cookbook. This book is for all of them.

INDEX

About the Author and Photographer

Megha Kohli is the Chef Partner at Mezze Mambo, a Mediterranean restaurant in New Delhi. She also runs a boutique hospitality consultancy, helping restaurateurs turn their visions into reality. With 18 years of experience in the food industry, her career highlights include working at The Oberoi's Italian fine-dining restaurant, Travertino, and heading operations at establishments such as The Olive Beach and Lavaash by Saby. Megha's passion extends beyond the kitchen – she actively promotes sustainable cooking practices on global platforms. She was selected for the prestigious Cochran Fellowship Program by the U.S. Department of Agriculture, represented India at the EAT Forum in Stockholm and cooked at the United Nations Food and Agriculture Organization in Rome. She was honoured as the 'Times Chef of the Year' in 2020.

Anshika Varma is a food and documentary photographer with over 20 years of experience across commercial and editorial platforms. Her work engages with visual storytelling in the culinary and hospitality industries, where she works closely with restaurants, chefs, and brands as a photographer, stylist and creative director. Her images present food as a culmination of celebration and capture the layered relationships people share with it, while emphasising its cultural nuance and sensory detail. Anshika has worked on over 20 book projects featuring some of the top chefs in the country, translating culinary narratives into richly photographed editions. Her work has appeared in award-winning books, magazines, digital campaigns and video series. In addition to her commercial practice, she is also an artist, curator and publisher. She is the founder of Offset Projects, an initiative that supports contemporary photography and the evolving language of the photobook through exhibitions, mentorships and collaborative publishing. She is based in Delhi, India.

ISBN: 9789392130779

Published in India by
Roli Books Pvt Ltd, 2025
M-75, Greater Kailash-II Market
New Delhi - 110048, India
Ph: +91-11-40682000
E-mail: info@rolibooks.com
Website: www.rolibooks.com

Printed and bound in New Delhi, India.